D1609040

New England's
Historic Homes & Gardens

**GIFT OF
LAURA BREYER**

Union Park Press
Wellesley, MA 02481
www.unionparkpress.com

Printed in China
First Edition

© 2011 Kim Knox Beckius
Photography © William H. Johnson

Library of Congress Control Number: 2011930330
ISBN: 978-1-934598-08-5; 1-934598-08-9

Book and cover design by theBookDesigners

All rights reserved. No part of this publication may be copied, stored in a retrieval system, or transmitted in any form by any means electronic, mechanical, recording or otherwise, except brief extractions for the purpose of review; no part of this publication my be sold or hired without the written permission of the publisher.

Although the author and Union Park Press have taken all reasonable care in preparing this book, we make no warranty about the accuracy and completeness of its content and, to the maximum extent permitted, disclaim all liability arising from its use.

All information in this book was accurate at the time of publication but is subject to change.

Union Park Press titles are also available in a variety of digital formats. Please visit our website to learn more: www.unionparkpress.com.

On the front cover: Glebe House, Woodbury, CT. *Frontispiece image:* Lockwood-Mathews Mansion Museum, Norwalk, CT. *Acknowledgements image:* Moffatt-Ladd House & Garden, Portsmouth, NH. *Introduction:* Eolia Mansion at Harkness Memorial State Park, Waterford, CT; and Lockwood-Mathews Mansion Museum, Norwalk, CT. *Image on pages 228-229:* Henry Whitfield House, Guilford, CT. *On the back cover, left to right:* Roseland Cottage, Woodstock, CT; Adams National Historic Park, Quincy, MA; Park-McCullough House, North Bennington, VT; Whitfield House, Guilford, CT.

New England's
Historic Homes & Gardens

Text by
KIM KNOX BECKIUS

Photography by
WILLIAM H. JOHNSON

UNION
PARK
PRESS

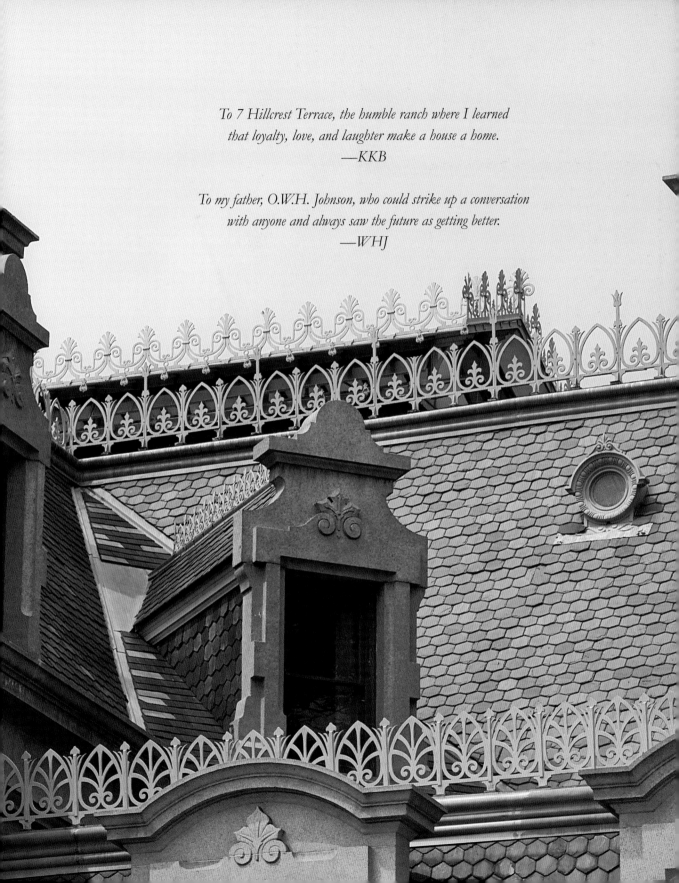

To 7 Hillcrest Terrace, the humble ranch where I learned
that loyalty, love, and laughter make a house a home.
—KKB

To my father, O.W.H. Johnson, who could strike up a conversation
with anyone and always saw the future as getting better.
—WHJ

Acknowledgments

I was impressed by so many of the passionate and knowledgeable docents, volunteers, gardeners, and site administrators who I encountered during my tours of these thirty-six historic treasures. I owe special thanks for arranging my travel and visits to Andrea Carneiro, Communications Manager, the Preservation Society of Newport County; Morgan Devlin, Marketing and Public Relations Manager, Newport Restoration Foundation; Stephanie Seacord, Leading Edge; Sandy Severance, President, Kennebunkport Historical Society; Peggy Wishart, Site Manager, Hamilton House, Historic New England; and Susan Wissler, Executive Director, The Mount.

I am grateful to my dad, George Snyder, for his thoughtful review of this manuscript, and to Union Park Press publisher Nicole Vecchiotti for her enthusiastic adoption of this project. I'm indebted, as well, to friends and family members who traveled with me as I researched this book, including Jessica Mand, Karin Oloffson, Dad, and my husband, Bruce, and daughter, Lara. Years ago, when I contemplated pursuing a PhD in history, my professor and mentor, the late Dr. William Olson, shared priceless advice: Do something lucrative instead. I am aware every day of how fortunate I am to earn a living traveling the historic roads of this incomparable region with the cherished people who make my life a joy by my side.

—*Kim Knox Beckius*

I would like to acknowledge all the volunteers and staff at all the historic homes who work to keep history alive. As Robert Heinlein said, "A generation which ignores history has no past and no future."

—*William H. Johnson*

Contents

Introduction

From the region's oldest surviving stone home, built in 1639, to a seaside granite castle that epitomizes twentieth-century Yankee ingenuity, from a royal governor's stately forty-room farmhouse to the palatial seventy-room mansion built for a nineteenth-century captain of industry—New England's historic houses trace the evolution of American architecture from days when the availability of natural materials and the quest for protection against both adversaries and an unbearably harsh climate dictated design to a time when immense wealth was monumentalized in elaborate structures lavish beyond colonial settlers' wildest imaginings. Hundreds of New England homes have been deemed worthy of preservation and interpretation: they offer insight into four centuries of American style and sensibility. Yet, with this architectural treasure trove comes immense responsibility.

Justifications for preservation are many and varied. While some of these landmark residences are outstanding examples of architectural artistry and period design elements, the mystique of most transcends the mere interplay of bricks, stone, mortar, plaster, wood, shingles, textiles, and glass. Each home bore witness to a succession of human dramas; each reflects its occupants' passions and pursuits. Within this six-state region, you'll find the humble homes of presidents and patriots, whose decisions and actions reverberate through time, and the wondrous lairs of capitalist barons, upon whom the fates thrust inconceivable riches but denied lasting notoriety. Most poignant are the edifices that sheltered individuals who appeared to have it all—LeGrand Lockwood, Thomas Plant, Edith Wharton, Doris Duke, Henry Wadsworth Longfellow, Mark Twain—for within these intimate spaces, their personal heartaches and misfortunes are revealed.

In considering a field of nearly one hundred notable homes for this volume, geographic and chronologic diversity were taken into account. Each contender was thoughtfully evaluated for its architectural and historic significance, its visual splendor, its popularity, its singularity, and its story. The end goal was to strike a balance, featuring landmarks of indisputable merit along with lesser known homes worthy of attention. Our years of traveling New England's byways in search of its most evocative images and its richest narratives have given each of us unique insights, and decision-making was not without lively debate. Ultimately, selecting the thirty-six New England houses and gardens most worthy of description and depiction required analysis of the chief factors that motivate prospective visitors. Some have genealogical interests or seek ideas as they refurbish their own antique homes. Art lovers are drawn to houses with museum-quality collections, architecture enthusiasts to opportunities to view exquisite construction and equally fine restoration work. Many travelers are drawn to scenic vistas and inspiring landscapes. Others are driven by simple curiosity: How extraordinary, after all, to stand upon the floorboards where Calvin Coolidge was born … or where Ulysses S. Grant bowled a strike.

True old home aficionados, however, understand that history is more than a litany of cold, dry facts and a timeline of unrelated events. It is a fascinating saga, and to stand within the walls that witnessed profound moments and mundane daily occurrences long ago is to be fully immersed in the human condition and touched by the common threads of emotion we all share. A three-dimensional portrait of pivotal characters in our nation's political and cultural development unfolds as you behold the spaces they once occupied and the possessions they cherished. Sure, Paul Revere was a rabble-rouser, but he was also a hardworking father with an awfully large brood. He sold his inflammatory engravings—and even moonlighted as a dentist—as much to keep food on the table as to stir the political pot. John Adams may have been cantankerous, but to peer at the bed he could never return to following the death of his lifelong love, Abigail, is to sense a softer side. And a chill sweeps over those who take in the view from the stand-up desk in Nathaniel Hawthorne's tower study, where the author continued to labor, too riddled with cancer to sit comfortably, too burdened with tales to put down his pen.

We endeavored to choose three dozen residences with the power to move and inspire all who step across their thresholds. The best reason to consider a historic home visit is, however, a selfless one. Maintained by a variety of not-for-profit organizations, historical societies, state and local groups, and even the National Park Service, they are in varying states of upkeep. While some appear beautifully maintained, others are unfurnished, water damaged, or desperately in need of fresh paint. The Mount—Wharton's Berkshires retreat—narrowly escaped foreclosure in 2008, and as of 2011, still needs to raise a large sum to meet loan obligations. For all their diversity, these fragile properties share one compelling denominator: a need for continual sources of funding. From scavenger hunts for children to indoor and outdoor art displays, many strive in this digital age to shake off their reputation as old, dusty, boring places. Every admission paid, every gift shop souvenir purchased, all donations large and small help to sustain these living links to our collective past.

For, as Twain presciently observed in 1896, structures forever bear the imprint of those who call them home. "To us, our house was not unsentient matter—it had a heart, and a soul, and eyes to see us with; and approvals, and solicitudes, and deep sympathies; it was of us, and we were in its confidence, and lived in its grace and in the peace of its benediction," he said. "We never came home from an absence that its face did not light up and speak out its eloquent welcome—and we could not enter it unmoved."

Part I

Connecticut

Lockwood-Mathews Mansion Museum

295 West Avenue • Norwalk, CT 06850 • 203-838-9799
www.lockwoodmathewsmansion.com

The 2004 remake of *The Stepford Wives* was a box office flop, but for the Lockwood-Mathews Mansion, one of several Connecticut filming locations, it was a blockbuster. Income and attention generated by the movie revved up conservation, restoration, and acquisition efforts at this magnificent home, where soaring heights, devastating blows, and cliffhangers were part of the script long before Hollywood came to town.

Norwalk native LeGrand Lockwood's Elm Park, the first significant post–Civil War estate, was built at a cost of two million dollars from 1864 to 1868. Designed by Paris-trained architect Detlef Lienau and touted to be one of the earliest and finest surviving examples of Second Empire style, the sixty-two-room country manor with indoor plumbing, a geothermal cooling system, and a basement bowling alley was intended to serve as a summer retreat for Wall Street financier Lockwood and his family. It certainly wasn't conceived for the role it would play in the 1940s and '50s, when it housed municipal offices and equipment: lawn mowers, voting machines, snow plows.

How did this lavish mansion, with décor by a who's who of the nineteenth century's leading interior designers, art by Hudson River School masters, and woodwork meticulously carved and inlaid by artisans from both sides of the Atlantic, befall such a fate? Just one year after the Lockwoods settled in, they suffered an irrecoverable reversal of fortune in the 1869 market crash precipitated by gold speculators. When LeGrand succumbed to pneumonia in 1872, he was just one ninety-thousand-dollar payment away from satisfying creditors. His widow, Ann Louisa, auctioned the home's contents but could not forestall foreclosure.

Charles D. Mathews, a wealthy retired New York provision dealer, and his wife, Rebecca, purchased the thirty-acre property in 1876, and it remained in their family until daughter Florence's death in 1938. The Mathewses were faithful stewards of the home. They reacquired many original furnishings and, when that proved impossible, commissioned new pieces to blend with each room's exactingly themed details.

When the City of Norwalk bought the estate in 1941, it had more sinister plans for the mansion than utilizing it as a storehouse. The four-story Victorian was targeted for demolition to make way for a modern municipal center. Heroic citizens, however, formed the non-profit Lockwood-Mathews Mansion Museum, Inc., to rescue the once-glorious dwelling from the brink.

Visitors who tour the home early April through early January see the results of a concerted push in the 2000s to recapture the interior's mid-nineteenth-century elegance via cinematic and curatorial magic. The rotunda—a gallery-like two-story space at the heart of the structure, with a parquet floor, soaring forty-two-foot ceiling, and a double skylight—got a fresh coat of carnelian paint and enormous landscape reproductions courtesy of Paramount Pictures. Although some liberties were taken during the rotunda's transformation to movie set, the effect clearly resembles the Lockwood-era appearance of this octagonal hall, where Albert Bierstadt's *The Domes of the Yosemite* once hung alongside paintings by Thomas Cole and Frederic Church. Commissioned by Lockwood for twenty-five thousand dollars

and sold by his wife for a mere fifty-one hundred, the Bierstadt—now worth many millions—is the centerpiece of the collection at Vermont's St. Johnsbury Athenaeum. While its return to Norwalk is inconceivable, a surprising number of Lockwood and Mathews possessions have been recouped considering Ann Louisa's disposition of its contents and the souvenir-taking that transpired during the 1940s and '50s.

While it is especially evident on the second floor that restoration remains a work in progress, visitors need only glance at black-and-white photographs displayed in each first-floor room to appreciate how faithfully curators have turned back the clock. Lockwood's cherished Joseph Mozier statues of Pocahontas and the *Wept of Wish-Ton-Wish* reassumed their rightful place in the marble-columned entrance hall in 2003. In 2008, acclaimed restoration expert John Canning oversaw conservation of the painted ceiling and woodwork in the Leon Marcotte—designed Italian Renaissance Revival—style library. In the French-inspired drawing room, with its ceiling canvas of *Venus at Play with Her Cupids* by Pierre-Victor Galland and furnishings custom-crafted by the prestigious nineteenth-century firm Herter Brothers, a Randolph Rogers sculpture of Edwin and Florence Lockwood, two of the Lockwoods' eight children, was a gift from Florence's grandson. Optimism reigns that additional treasures will resurface. The chances are decidedly better than those for a *Stepford Wives II*.

Henry Whitfield House

248 Old Whitfield Street • Guilford, CT 06437 • 203-453-2457 •
www.ct.gov; Search: Henry Whitfield

ike the Pilgrims, Reverend Henry Whitfield's Puritan followers fled England in 1639 so they might worship freely on America's shores. Their six-week Atlantic crossing landed them in New Haven, and after acquiring nearby parcels from the Menuncatuck tribe, they established a primitive settlement ringing the spacious green that is still Guilford's centerpiece. Most congregants built wood-frame, thatch-roof, one- or two-room homes. Whitfield was one of four community leaders obliged to erect a fortress-like stone structure where the others might retreat if faced with threats from the natives, the Dutch, or the Crown. The Henry Whitfield House never came under attack, but Connecticut's oldest home has stood through hurricanes and nor'easters, the interpersonal dramas of countless inhabitants, and nearly four centuries of political, social, and economic evolution.

The oldest surviving stone home in New England is as enigmatic as it is enduring. Few records of the structure exist prior to 1830, and while archaeological digs conducted by Yale University students from 2000 to 2007 unearthed shards and fragments galore, few intact artifacts were found. The residence was likely sparsely furnished and rather cave-like when it sheltered the minister, his wife Dorothy, seven children, and indentured servants.

Subsequent owners rented the property to a succession of tenant farmers whose names and undertakings have been largely lost to history. Yet, Guilford residents remained keenly aware of the structure's significance, and members of the Connecticut Society of the Colonial Dames of America began petitioning the state to preserve this architectural anomaly in 1897. The state purchased the site in 1900 and created the Henry Whitfield State Historical Museum to serve as a collections repository. Architectural historian Norman Isham was hired in 1903 to begin restoration. While the goal was to open up exhibit space, as Reverend William G. Andrews told the

New Haven Colony Historical Society when the museum debuted in 1904, "To destroy anything ancient in constructing a room intended for the reception and preservation of ancient things would have been as absurd as it would have been monstrous."

As the Colonial Revival movement matured in the 1930s, architect J. Frederick Kelly tackled an extensively researched, Works Progress Administration–funded restoration aimed at returning the Whitfield House to its 1639 appearance. Only the exterior granite walls were determined to be original; the rest of the house was reconstructed based on physical evidence and a study of similarly styled houses in northern England.

On self-guided tours, offered early May through October, visitors discover that this three-story relic still houses a diverse assemblage of artifacts. There are more chests on display than the entire community possessed in 1639. Like most Colonial Revival–period restorations, the site glorifies America's heritage and traditions. Visitors are even allowed to poke around in the attic, where cabinets of curiosities are filled with items that run the gamut from Revolutionary War powder horns and uniforms to late eighteenth-century and early nineteenth-century clothing. The one-handed clock from Guilford's First Congregational Church—crafted by Ebenezer Parmelee in 1726 and reputed to be the first steeple clock made in the colonies—is also on view. Early Americans had little need to tell time to the exact minute.

In a house this old, it's likewise of little consequence that knowledge of the events that transpired within these stone walls is inexact. What resonates is the structure's resilience, especially when contrasted with that of the man whose name it bears. Whitfield—who first roused the Anglican Church's ire by refusing to read from the *Book of Sports* condoning recreation on the Sabbath—proved too fragile for New England's rigors. In *A General History of New England*, written in 1680 and published in 1814, William Hubbard reveals: "After sundry years continuance in the country, he found it too difficult for him, partly from the sharpness of the air, he having a weak body, and partly from the toughness of those employments wherein his livelihood was to be sought, he having been tenderly and delicately brought up." By 1650, religious intolerance had ebbed, and Whitfield hightailed it back to England.

Eolia Mansion at Harkness Memorial State Park

275 Great Neck Road • Waterford, CT 06385 • 860-443-5725
www.ct.gov; Search: Harkness

Eolia, named for Aeolus—Greek keeper of the winds—was designed by New York architects Lord & Hewlett for William and Jessie Stillman Taylor. Within a year after its completion in 1906, however, Jessie decided the forty-two-room Italianate villa on Long Island Sound simply didn't suit her. Seeing an opportunity in her sister's buyer's remorse, Mary Stillman Harkness and her husband, Edward, added the estate to their collection of six homes, including a mansion on Manhattan's Fifth Avenue. The winds of financial fortune had blessed the Harknesses, who inherited vast riches that Edward's father amassed as the second largest shareholder in John D. Rockefeller's Standard Oil. For all they possessed, however, Mary and Edward lacked one thing they desperately desired, and their legacy lies in what they gave away: more than two hundred million dollars during their lifetimes and a trove of treasures after their deaths, including this 230-acre seaside jewel.

The high-ceilinged rooms on the first floor of the mansion, open for tours on weekends and holidays Memorial Day weekend through Labor Day, are devoid of furnishings. The Harknesses, who spent their honeymoon on an Egyptian dig, donated many of the artifacts and works of art that graced their Connecticut home to museums. Still, visitors sense the dwelling's bygone grandeur thanks to black-and-white historic photographs and surviving architectural details, such as the floral-painted dining room ceiling. Second-floor bedrooms are decorated to reflect their early twentieth-century appearance: One is an exhibition space highlighting the couple's interests.

Unlike wealthy contemporaries, who entertained lavishly, the Harknesses were reserved, private, and—above all—philanthropic. In addition to donating hefty sums to universities

and hospitals, the reluctantly childless couple brought New York City children stricken with polio and tuberculosis to the Connecticut shore each April through October and provided for their care and recreation. On the Fourth of July—Mrs. Harkness's birthday—each child received a gift, and their families were not only transported via private railroad car to the celebration but also were reimbursed by their hosts for lost wages. When Mary died in 1950—ten years after Edward—she bequeathed Eolia to the state of Connecticut and also ensured the perpetuity of Camp Harkness, which offers free therapeutic and recreational summer programs to Connecticut youngsters with physical and intellectual disabilities.

Although the state's ability to finance restoration efforts at the park is limited, much has been accomplished by the Friends of Harkness, a non-profit group that coordinates fundraising and revenue-generating site rentals. The stunning gardens and grounds—open daily year-round—are testament to the generous spirit that endures here as steadfastly as saltwater breezes. Devoted volunteers maintain the elaborate and innovative planting schemes devised by prominent landscape gardener Beatrix Farrand, the lone woman among the founders of the American Society of Landscape Architects. Hired by the Harknesses in 1918 to expand upon and revise Brett & Hall's landscape plan, Farrand first lent her touch to the West Garden, with its wisteria- and grapevine-draped Neoclassical pergola designed by architect James Gamble Rogers, who also remodeled the mansion's interior and drew plans for the carriage house—complete with a bowling alley, billiard room, squash court, and turntable that facilitated parking of nine limousines. Farrand shaped the property for more than a decade, adding the Oriental-themed East Garden, with its stone Foo dog gatekeepers, a geometric boxwood parterre, cutting gardens that supplied fresh flowers for each room, and a tangled red-leafed cluster of Japanese maples with room enough inside for grown-ups to hide. Farrand's finale, an Alpine Rock Garden inspired by her coastal Maine childhood, serves as a graceful segue between the cultivated landscape and the sea.

Harkness Memorial State Park not only preserves this rare surviving example of Farrand's work, it stands as a reminder that life's gifts are not to be taken for granted. The Harknesses viewed wealth as more responsibility than entitlement. Mary wrote in a 1939 letter to the president of Connecticut College, one of many beneficiaries of their largesse, "It is always a lottery to know just how things are going to turn out."

The Glebe House Museum &
The Gertrude Jekyll Garden

49 Hollow Road • Woodbury, CT 06798 • 203-263-2855
www.theglebehouse.org

Prolific and influential garden designer and author Gertrude Jekyll never traveled across the pond, yet her notion of how plantings should gracefully complement the homes they enfold, her knack for interweaving botanical splashes of color and texture to create a painterly scene, and her conviction that horticulture is equal parts fine art and practical science all spring from theory to vivid reality in Connecticut. Wildly popular in her native England and credited with more than four hundred European gardens, Jekyll only undertook three U.S. commissions, and the gardens she planned for the Glebe House in 1926 are the only surviving American example of her work—even though they were not installed as planned.

Why Jekyll's sketches were abandoned is something of a mystery. Perhaps the nation's plummet into the Great Depression was to blame. The sketches were drawn based on photographs at the request of Standard Oil heiress and Glebe House benefactress Annie Burr Jennings the year after the colonial dwelling opened as a house museum. When Jekyll's long forgotten design was discovered in 1978 by a University of Connecticut student researching her master's thesis, however, executing Jekyll's vision became a tantalizing possibility. Planting began in 1990, more than a half century after the noted designer's death. And while some modifications were necessary because prescribed plant varieties were no longer available or too fragile to withstand New England's climate, the six-hundred-foot English-style

mixed border, lush planted stone terrace, and rose allée are signature Jekyll creations perfectly befitting the architectural gem they enhance.

Less of a mystery is why Jennings and fellow founding members of the Seabury Society for the Preservation of the Glebe House endeavored to save the 1750 structure, considered the Episcopal Church's birthplace in the New World. *Glebe* is an Old English word for cultivable, parish-owned land, and this rural tract became home in 1771 to Woodbury's first permanent Anglican minister, his wife, and their family, which grew to nine children, even as life became rather uncomfortable. Automatically considered royal sympathizers, most Anglican ministers returned to England or fled to Canada as revolutionary sentiment swelled,

but Reverend John Rutgers Marshall persevered, even though he was harassed by local militia and essentially under house arrest Monday through Saturday. The secret meeting Marshall hosted on March 25, 1783, at which he and nine fellow clergymen selected Samuel Seabury to serve as America's first Episcopal bishop, cemented the Glebe House's place in church history.

The modest farmhouse, elegant by colonial standards, has a unique roofline that combines gambrel and saltbox styles. Inside, visitors see the concealed sliding panel through which Marshall often escaped to the basement to avoid arrest, even though he was as American as he was devout. Also displayed are family possessions, including a Bible, the trunk Seabury packed for his transatlantic voyage to seek ordination

as bishop, and collected period pieces. Highlights include three highboys by local craftsman Elijah Booth and an eclectic array of kitchen implements, from pewter plates and a cauldron for making soap and washing clothes to an antique mouse trap and a portable grill for cooking in the woods.

It is rare for a historic home to be best known for its late twentieth-century additions. Most preservationists are inclined to reverse or camouflage modern accoutrements. Yet the society, which offers tours May through November, embraces its dual stewardship of one of America's earliest house museums and the flowering frame in which it has been set. "A garden is a grand teacher. It teaches patience and careful watchfulness ... above all it teaches entire trust," Jekyll once wrote. The Glebe

House's gardens are a dynamic, evolving, ongoing experiment that requires constant attention, but this leap of faith has earned the site an expanded audience of supporters and visitors captivated and inspired by the pioneering horticulturalist's Impressionistic schemes, pleasing palette, and surprising juxtapositions. "The lesson I have thoroughly learnt, and wish to pass on to others," Jekyll reflected, "is to know the enduring happiness that the love of a garden gives." Those who care for and cherish this rare reincarnation of her work ensure Jekyll's passion persists in the unlikeliest of places.

The Mark Twain
House & Museum

351 Farmington Avenue • Hartford, CT 06105 • 860-247-0998
www.marktwainhouse.org

He grew up in Hannibal, Missouri; worked as a printer in New York, Philadelphia, and Cincinnati; went west—and to Europe—in pursuit of a journalism career following a stint as a steamboat pilot on the Mississippi; and is buried beside the love of his life in her hometown, Elmira, New York. Yet Samuel Langhorne Clemens—better known as Mark Twain—spent his happiest, most prolific chapter embracing his adopted identity: Connecticut Yankee.

"You do not know what beauty is if you have not been here," Twain wrote of Hartford following his first visit in 1868 at the behest of the publisher of his first successful tome, *The Innocents Abroad*. Hartford soon became the Clemenses' home, and the brick Victorian they built in 1874 at Nook Farm, a literary enclave on the city's outskirts where neighbors included Harriet Beecher Stowe, nurtured not only a growing family but an imaginative cast of characters who would outlive them all. During his seventeen years in Hartford, Twain penned eight major works, including his most enduring and acclaimed tales *The Adventures of Tom Sawyer*, *The Prince and the Pauper*, *Adventures of Huckleberry Finn*, and *A Connecticut Yankee in King Arthur's Court*.

Twain sketched a floor plan accentuating views of the rural countryside and now-subterranean Park River, and New York architect Edward Tuckerman Potter designed the nineteen-room Victorian Gothic with Stick style influences. Built with wife Olivia's inheritance, the elaborate interior décor—conceived by Louis Comfort Tiffany's firm Associated Artists—had to wait until 1881, after *Tom Sawyer* royalties poured in. An enlarged kitchen and servants' wing, which visitors can view on a separate tour, was also added at this time. Among modern conveniences was one of the first telephones installed in a private home. The author diligently

noted artillery-like static and other complaints in a log submitted to the telephone company with each duly adjusted bill.

Twain was more of a Renaissance man than many recognize. While writing and speaking earned him fame, he pursued other shortcuts to fortune, trying his hand at everything from mining to patenting inventions, including a self-pasting scrapbook. But he was a colossal failure when it came to business investments. In the museum, visitors behold one of only two Paige compositors manufactured. Twain sunk nearly two hundred thousand dollars into the Betamax of typesetting machines: a nine-thousand-pound clunker with eighteen thousand movable parts. By 1891, the Clemenses were so deeply in debt, they shuttered their Farmington Avenue residence and moved abroad. Lecture tour earnings enabled Twain to settle his accounts and return to the United States in 1900.

The family could not bear, however, to return to Hartford. Eldest daughter Susy had perished of meningitis in the home during a return visit in 1896. The property was sold in 1903 and served as a boys' school and apartment building before efforts to save it were initiated in 1919. By 1929, the state-chartered Mark Twain Memorial and Library Commission had purchased the house, but it was utilized as a public library until sufficient funds were raised to begin restoration in 1955.

Open year-round for tours, including Victorian-themed holiday walkthroughs, Twain's refuge remains a work in progress.

Photographic and written records, along with physical evidence, have enabled restoration carpenters and stencil-work painters to turn the clock back to the period from 1881 to 1891, and curators have refurnished the home with family possessions and period pieces. It is easy to envision Twain pacing around the dining room table, trying out his latest zingers on guests; daughters Susy, Clara, and Jean studying and practicing piano in the schoolroom or entertaining their father with plays staged against the backdrop of the library and its lush conservatory; the brilliant author splaying pages of prose across the billiard table in his third-floor writing retreat; and Sam and Livy settling in with their feet at the headboard of their Venetian angel bed so they might view its elaborately carved cherubs.

Only Clara survived her father: It fell to her to protect his literary legacy. Though there was little doubt his works would be cherished by future generations, the family's Hartford habitat faced less certain longevity. The foresight of locals who strove to protect this landmark ensures there will always be a place to appreciate the triumphs and tragedies of an American icon, whose words of wisdom ring true and tickle funny bones across the ages.

Roseland Cottage

556 Route 169 • Woodstock, CT 06281 • 860-928-4074
www.historicnewengland.org; Search: Roseland

From 1870 to 1895, America's most extravagant Fourth of July celebrations transpired against a backdrop of red, white, blue—and pink. Roseland Cottage, the Gothic Revival showpiece Henry Chandler Bowen built in 1846 on the green in his native Woodstock, has worn a palette of thirteen rosy hues from sandstone to sherbet, but the Pink House and its gracious grounds were festooned with patriotic bunting, flags, and lanterns each July as the nation's political leaders and literati toasted independence with pink lemonade.

How was Mr. Fourth of July, as the teetotaling Bowen became known, able to lure luminaries to his summer home in this bucolic corner of Connecticut? Born a shopkeeper's son in the town where his family settled in 1776, Bowen left Woodstock at twenty-one for New York City. After five years as a store clerk, he and a colleague launched their own shop. By the time that business failed on the eve of the Civil War, Bowen had already married his former employer's daughter, Lucy Tappan; parlayed his earnings into successful investments, including a controlling interest in leading abolitionist newspaper the *New York Independent*; and played a pivotal role in founding the Republican Party and championing its first successful presidential candidate, Abraham Lincoln.

Bowen's ardent Republican support and influential role as publisher made it unwise to decline invitations to attend his July 3 galas and to speak at July 4 festivities lavished on his rural neighbors. Among his storied guests were four men who held the nation's highest office: Ulysses S. Grant, Rutherford B. Hayes, Benjamin Harrison,

and William McKinley. It's as easy to imagine Grant's consternation at being required by his virtuous host to smoke his cigars in the garden as it is to envision the president's elation at throwing a strike with his first ball. Visitors can still see the nation's oldest indoor bowling alley inside the carriage barn.

Although the bunting has long since been stored away, Roseland Cottage, named for Bowen's favorite flower, has been restored to its 1880s heyday, and it stands as a quintessential example of the aesthetic principles espoused by the nineteenth century's most influential architectural pundit. Although credit for the nineteen-room structure's design goes to Joseph C. Wells, it is evident that Bowen was a devotee of Andrew Jackson Downing, whose ideals imbue the estate. In addition to the barn and gabled main house, with its vertical board-and-batten siding, lattice windows, and terracotta chimney pots, several outbuildings—including the garden house and privy—also survive, making the Bowen home a rare complete example of a planned mid-Victorian estate exemplifying Downing's emphasis on the harmonious interplay between structures and their surroundings.

The mansion's contents, including Gothic furnishings attributed to Brooklyn craftsman Thomas Brooks, are original with the exception of a single rug, and on tours offered June through October 15, visitors are immersed in this dark cathedral-like interior. Newly invented, intricately embossed

Lincrusta-Walton wallcoverings installed in the 1880s have proven surprisingly durable. Jewel-toned stained glass allows glints of colored light to penetrate the home's formality.

When viewed from the second floor, the Victorian boxwood parterre garden mimics these stained glass forms. Installed in 1850 at a cost of five hundred and fifty dollars for plants and labor, including six hundred yards of boxwood hedge, the garden's curvaceous shrubbery and pathways outline twenty-one flower beds, which staff and volunteers plant each year with more than four thousand annuals according to the original plan. The Downing-inspired layout features concentrations of color, and the spectrum of historic specimens blooms from early spring through late autumn.

Bowen also oversaw development of lakeshore Roseland Park, which he left in trust to the public. At the 1875 Woodstock Fair, he counseled neighbors: "You can at least plant an elm or a rosebush every year, and you will not have lived entirely in vain." After the patriarch's death in 1896 at the age of eighty-three, a trio of his children lived at Roseland Cottage year-round. Granddaughter Constance Holt, the final descendant to occupy the house, died in 1968, and in 1970, Historic New England acquired one of the best preserved and documented Gothic Revival estates in America. In the annals of history, Bowen's career may be a footnote, but he'd be tickled pink that his passion for independence and simple virtue live on in his hometown.

Part II
Rhode Island

Gilbert Stuart
Birthplace and Museum

815 Gilbert Stuart Road • Saunderstown, RI 02874 • 401-294-3001
www.gilbertstuartmuseum.com

His artwork is regularly crumpled and creased, exchanged for cheap merchandise, wadded, and inadvertently run through the wash. Yet his paintings have also fetched millions and hang in America's most exalted museums, and his humble birthplace, situated on the picturesque banks of Mattatuxet Brook, is a National Historic Landmark.

Gilbert Stuart committed to canvas—and to Americans' collective conscious—the iconic features and expressions of early America's foremost figures. Of the more than one thousand portraits he painted, however, none is more enduring and ubiquitous than the unfinished bust of George Washington, which he painted from life in 1796 and used as a model for subsequent depictions of the first president. Known as the Athenaeum portrait, it graces the United States' most circulated currency: the one-dollar bill.

Although he did not demonstrate artistic promise until after his family moved to Newport, Rhode Island, the gambrel-roofed home where Stuart spent his first seven years celebrates

his prolificity and celebrity. Built in 1751, it also stands as a finely restored example of residential and industrial colonial construction. Inside the Common Room, a multipurpose space with wide plank floors and hand-hewn beams occupying the entire first floor, visitors see not only a brick hearth and beehive oven, a cobbler's bench, and an enormous weaving loom, but the exposed mechanics of a recreation of America's

first snuff mill. Stuart's father, a Scottish immigrant, launched his tobacco-grinding enterprise with two local partners. Long before the advent of television, the water-wheel-powered mill's perpetual movement must have provided background noise and visual interest for the self-sufficient family.

Up a claustrophobic staircase, the second story, which is level with the mill pond and woods at the rear of the property, has two bedrooms and a keeping room, each with a distinctive corner fireplace. Furnishings in the home, such as the Birth Room's deerskin trunk, cradle, and tripod candle stand, are period antiques, although none belonged to the family. Reproductions of the artist's most famous portraits grace the walls, offering a sense not only of his mastery of the genre but of the influential circles in which he moved. John Adams said of Stuart, who was known for setting paints to canvas without first sketching his subjects: "Speaking generally, no penance is like having one's picture done. You must sit in a constrained and unnatural position, which is a trial to the temper. But I should like to sit to Stuart from the first of January to the last of December, for he lets me do just what I please, and keeps me constantly amused by his conversation."

The Gilbert Stuart Birthplace—one of more than a dozen structures restored by architectural historian and Brown University professor Norman Isham—opened as a

George Washington by Gilbert Stuart
Oil on Canvas 96" x 64"
State of Rhode Island and Providence Plantations

This portrait is one of two identical portraits of George
Washington ordered by the Rhode Island General
Assembly in February 1800. On March 2, 1802, the
pictures were delivered: one to the Old Colony House in
Newport, where it still hangs, and this one to the Old
State House on Benefit Street in Providence, where it
hung until 1901 when it was moved to the new State
House to hang in the State Reception Room.

Gift of Carol and Bob Bresler

museum in 1930. In 2007, the 1662 gristmill was relocated to the site and returned to working order more than a century after it last produced cornmeal for the state's signature johnnycakes. Although the gristmill operates just twice annually, at special spring and fall events, and tours of the house and colonial herb garden are only offered from early May through mid-October, the scenic grounds and woodland walking trails are accessible year-round. In early spring, nature lovers and ravenous birds are attracted by the annual return of tens of thousands of spawning-minded river herring that wriggle their way up a fish ladder, installed by the Rhode Island Department of Environmental Management, to Pausacaco Pond, perpetuating the property's status as a notable birthplace.

Blithewold Mansion, Gardens & Arboretum

101 Ferry Road • Bristol, RI 02809 • 401-253-2707
www.blithewold.org

The fifty thousand cheery daffodils that erupt in an undulating carpet of yellow and white along the pathways of Blithewold's North Garden each spring belie the tragic events experienced by this seaside estate's owners. Augustus Van Wickle, heir to his father's Pennsylvania coal mining business, purchased seventy acres on Narragansett Bay in 1894 while vacationing in the state he'd become enchanted with as a Brown University student. He hadn't intended to purchase a summer place … until he impulsively acquired a seventy-two-foot Herreshoff yacht and needed a spot to dock it. In 1896, a wood-shingled Queen Anne Victorian designed by Hoppin & Koen was completed, but Augustus enjoyed only two summers here before mortally wounding himself while skeet-shooting, five months before his second daughter's birth.

Bessie Pardee Van Wickle, a coal baron's daughter, remarried Augustus's old chum William McKee in 1901 and continued to summer at Blithewold with daughters Marjorie and Augustine, but in 1906, misfortune revisited when hoses could not reach a slow-burning fire between the roof and third floor. The mansion's contents—furniture, china, rugs, even bathtubs—were scattered across the lawn as the structure succumbed. As resilient as the sunny blossoms that awaken each April, Bessie lost no time hiring Boston architects

Kilham and Hopkins to design a grander, more fire-resistant dwelling at the hub of the landscape she'd begun shaping with the aid of New York City parks superintendent John De Wolf. The new Blithewold, a forty-five-room English country–style stone manor, capitalized on surrounding views and summoned the outdoors in.

Passionate travelers and collectors, the McKees filled their abode with antiques and reproductions—anything that caught their eye and exuded casual elegance—yet the eclectic scheme mindfully blends periods and styles. Little has changed since Bessie decorated in 1910, largely because another catastrophe—this time financial—befell the family when William's leather wholesaling business, which he had shored up with Bessie's inheritance, failed following the 1929 crash. The billiard room, with its sunset views, has both seventeenth-century Italian oak and leather armchairs and a rosewood and oak pool table crafted circa 1900, when the pastime was all the rage. A seventeenth-century Dutch cabinet is tucked into a corner of the living room, where the 1910 Chickering piano and 1925 Victrola also seem perfectly at home.

Blithewold's similarly diverse assemblage of trees—one of America's most unique arboreta—is reason alone for a visit. Among fifty significant specimens is a century-old Sargent's weeping hemlock; a rare flowering Franklin tree, which has not been sighted in the wild since 1803; a weeping European beech planted circa 1900; and a giant sequoia—Earth's most massive tree—transplanted from Brooklyn's Prospect Park by

De Wolf in 1911. At eighty-five feet, it is one of the tallest east of the Rockies. Marjorie Van Wickle Lyon, who shared her mother's horticultural flair, propagated sequoia seedlings and added a fragrant star magnolia and other leafy treasures.

With the Great Depression deepening and their fortunes irrevocably reversed, the McKees sought a buyer for Blithewold, appraised at ninety-five thousand dollars in 1932. Unsuccessful, they parted with their Boston home and took up year-round residence in Rhode Island. Marjorie sold off parcels to support the estate but retained ownership until her death in 1976 at age ninety-three, when the property was transferred to the non-profit Save Blithewold, Inc. Open mid-April through Columbus Day for mansion tours and daily year-round for those who would like to explore the grounds, Blithewold draws its largest crowds during Daffodil Days, when visitors can reserve afternoon tea in the dining room, as well as at Christmastime, when the mansion re-opens and a two-story tree dominates the balconied Colonial Revival–inspired center hall.

Bessie's love of lavish entertaining remains part of Blithewold's legacy, but it is the striking landscape she envisioned that more importantly endures. Although she lost a husband, a mansion, and vast riches, Bessie's dream for Blithewold, articulated in 1910, remains fulfilled a century later. "The plan was to create a park with distinctive features using the house as a center," she wrote. "And everywhere nature's bounteous gifts have served under man's skillful guidance to create an estate in which new beauties are constantly revealed and the perfect accord between architecture and grounds is ever apparent."

The Breakers

44 Ochre Point Avenue • Newport, RI 02840 • 401-847-1000
www.newportmansions.org

Named for its breathtaking setting overlooking the chiseled cliffs that rebuff the Atlantic's relentless assault, The Breakers is a true American palace. Completed in 1895 at the apex of an era when wealth—not birth—anointed a new American royalty, the 138,300-square-foot, seventy-room Italian Renaissance–style summer vacation home epitomizes Gilded Age excess. Constructed of Indiana limestone in just two years, based on Richard Morris Hunt's plans, the architecturally superb structure combined technical advances and innovative interpretations of classic European forms. No expense was spared by Cornelius Vanderbilt II, whose father, William Henry Vanderbilt, had doubled the $100 million fortune inherited from *his* father, self-made shipping and railroad tycoon Commodore Cornelius Vanderbilt. The sum—equivalent to four billion dollars today—made William Henry Vanderbilt the world's richest man, yet he viewed this fortune, bequeathed largely to eldest son Cornelius, as something of a burden. "The care of $200 million is too great a load for any back or brain to bear. It's enough to kill a man," he rued.

Inside The Breakers, where even clothes closets elicit admiring gasps, it is difficult to sympathize with the Vanderbilts' plight. The twenty-four-hundred-square-foot dining room, designed to dazzle fellow members of the Four Hundred—New York's social elite—gleams with gold leaf. Twin twelve-foot Baccarat crystal chandeliers illuminate a massive oak table surrounded by dozens of plush red damask chairs, and on the fifty-foot-high ceiling, a mythical figure drives a team of white steeds. The adjacent billiard room sports marble walls, alabaster arches, Tiffany sconces, and an intricate, symbolism-imbued mosaic ceiling and floor. The gray-green morning room, decorated by Jules Allard, has paintings of muses on its decadent, platinum leaf wall panels. The music room was a grandiose setting for soirees, including daughter Gertrude's marriage to Harry

Payne Whitney. The library's dark wood walls are stippled with gold leaf to achieve the look of tooled leather.

In contrast, second-floor bedrooms seem airy and sparse, reflecting the touch of decorator Ogden Codman, Jr., who advocated understated style. Most Newport summer cottages had a single bathroom: The Breakers had twenty. Mr. Vanderbilt's marble tub was so thick, servants were required to fill and drain it several times until it warmed. Four spacious closets housed Mrs. Vanderbilt's wardrobe: Newport women often changed their frocks seven times per day.

While most visitors can't fathom this opulent lifestyle, self-guided audio tours offered year-round breathe life into The Breakers and humanize its inhabitants, from the Vanderbilt grandchildren, who tricycled 'round the immense Great Hall and careened down grand staircase banisters on silver platters, to the immigrant servants, who grumbled about how much dusting was involved but kept the mansion and its oceanview gardens and grounds running like a well-oiled machine.

The unfolding of these stories evokes a modicum of empathy. Cornelius enjoyed only one healthy summer at The Breakers before suffering a stroke. He died in 1899

at age fifty-five. His wife, Alice, summered in Newport until her death thirty-five years later, when the mansion fell to youngest daughter Gladys Vanderbilt Széchenyi, who had wed a Hungarian count. Times had changed, however, and the "stately, ritualistic pattern" of life she cherished as a child had vanished. Her husband's death and the start of World War II prompted the countess to shutter The Breakers for a decade. In 1948, the home was opened for tours to raise funds for the Preservation Society of Newport County, which eventually purchased the property from Gladys's heirs in 1972 for less than four hundred thousand dollars.

The Breakers is filled with exquisite features, such as the John La Farge stained glass skylight, and the most magnificent treasures money could buy at the turn of the twentieth century, yet its significance transcends its contents and the prominence of its occupants. This grand edifice is emblematic of America's emergence as an industrial powerhouse and lead player on the world stage. Built during a complex time, when society was highly stratified, it nevertheless reflected pervasive national optimism stoked by captains of industry, whose conspicuous materialism signified the ultimate realization of the American Dream.

Rough Point

680 Bellevue Avenue • Newport, RI 02840 • 401-847-8344

www.newportrestoration.org

Reclusive, enigmatic heiress Doris Duke died in 1993 at age eighty. Seven years later, in accordance with her will, Rough Point's doors opened to the public, shedding captivating light on the penchants and passions of America's wealthiest woman. Sequestered between sea spray and stone walls, Doris's childhood summer home—one of five spectacular residences she owned—was a prized retreat during her final three decades. It remains essentially unaltered. The great hall's massive walls are adorned with museum-coveted masterpieces, while in the Morning Room, scattered throw pillows—gifts from friends—are embroidered with favorite wry quips like, "My decision is maybe and that's final."

The subject of intense fascination and speculation during her lifetime and of books and biopics after her death, James Buchanan Duke's only child was thrust into the public eye at age twelve when she inherited the tobacco and energy tycoon and Duke University benefactor's $100 million fortune and several homes, including Rough Point. Built from 1887 to 1891 for Frederick W. Vanderbilt, the sandstone and granite English manor on a waterfront plot landscaped by Frederick Law Olmsted was purchased by Duke in 1922. He died in 1925, one year after architect Horace Trumbauer remodeled and expanded the structure to thirty-nine thousand square feet.

Unlike her Bellevue Avenue neighbors, whose fortunes slumped, Doris made wise investments and saw her worth soar to more than one billion dollars. Stories swirled around the jet-setting, best-dressed, belly dancing, twice married, often indiscreet socialite, but at her Newport home, a more complex portrait emerges of a woman with highly developed talents and interests, a keen eye for design, diverse philanthropic missions, and a willingness to

gather debris from her storm-littered lawn dressed in jeans and a flannel shirt.

Of course, the mythology surrounding Ms. Duke wasn't entirely unfounded. Even rumors that she allowed pet camels inside the mansion at Rough Point were grounded in truth. During 1991's Hurricane Bob, Princess and Baby—acquired during negotiations to purchase an airplane from Arab sheiks—were indeed housed within the boarded-up solarium, where cracks in tall mirrors evince their agitation.

Throughout Doris's tenure, ten to twelve rescue dogs roamed Rough Point's interiors, which makes the impeccable condition of the dining room's pre-Ming dynasty baluster jars—the oldest pieces in the house—miraculous. Like her father, Doris adored fine art and furnishings: Rough Point was as much

a treasure trove as a home. Yet, the frequent gatherings she hosted while in residence May through November were casual affairs. In the oceanview dining room, where tapestries from three centuries adorn walls and screens, a life-sized Tiffany silver swan perches on the table, and a vivid old master painting looms over the mantel, Doris enjoyed gathering guests around a fire she'd started herself. In the music room, with its hand-painted eighteenth-century Chinese wallpaper, Chinese export porcelain pieces, and Louis XVI furniture upholstered with conversation-sparking fable scenes, the accomplished pianist improvised her own jazz compositions. And upstairs in Doris's boudoir, with its dazzling mother-of-pearl and ivory-inlaid furnishings and regal purple fabrics, accents include not only Renoir's

Young Girl Sewing but a hunk of driftwood reminiscent of a camel's head and trophies won for playing tennis and building sand castles long before the charitable foundation that bears her name began granting significant monetary awards to preservationists, medical researchers, dancers, and wildlife conservationists.

Tours of Rough Point, now under the auspices of the Newport Restoration Foundation, are offered from mid-April through early November, and while they leave most visitors agape, they only hint at Doris's mania for amassing extraordinary possessions. The wine cellar at Duke Farms in New Jersey held nearly two thousand rare pre–World War II bottles. Shangri-La, her Hawaiian hideaway, has a stunning array of Islamic art. Her jewelry fetched nearly twelve

million dollars at auction, and the couture fashions that flattered her tall, slender frame are periodically displayed at Rough Point, which was not the only Newport house she owned. Doris also snatched up nearly eighty colonial-era structures along the narrow, cobbled streets of this historic seaport. The Newport Restoration Foundation is equally devoted to preserving this architectural legacy, a generous bequest that ensures the character of Newport will forever reflect its eighteenth-century origins, as well as its age of excess.

Green Animals

380 Cory's Lane • Portsmouth, RI 02871 • 401-847-1000
www.newportmansions.org

Although the white clapboard Victorian cottage pales in scale and grandeur compared to other Preservation Society of Newport County–owned mansions in nearby Newport, the gardens at Green Animals are a work of shear artistry. Eighty topiary creations—including twenty-one whimsical creatures—are hand-trimmed with pruning shears using the same techniques that first brought them to life in the early decades of the twentieth century. One unfortunate misclip, and the elegant symmetry of a boxwood spiral might be irrevocably disturbed, the unicorn relegated to the rank of mere horse.

Sustaining the nation's oldest and northernmost topiary garden is a labor-intensive undertaking, but for visitors—especially children—this emerald animal city appears a product of enchantment. The tale of this circus of well-trained shrubbery begins in 1872 when Thomas E. Brayton, treasurer of the Union Cotton Manufacturing Company in Fall River, Massachusetts, purchased a gracious summer home and farm on seven acres sloping toward Narragansett Bay. Portuguese gardener Joseph Carreiro, who served as the property's superintendent from 1905 to 1945, was charged not only with cultivating herbs, fruits, and vegetables but with designing ornamental topiary and flower gardens. His imaginative living sculptures inspired Alice Brayton, who took up permanent residence in Portsmouth following her father's death in 1939, to christen the property Green Animals.

In 1945, Carreiro handed over his shears—and the job of superintendent—to his son-in-law and assistant George Mendonca, who tended and added to the glossy green menagerie. Even after his retirement in 1985, Mendonca continued to volunteer to clip and care for these playful pets and geometric shapes fashioned from California privet, English boxwood, and yew.

Alice, who loved entertaining guests at Green Animals, never married. Mendonca recalled in a 1997 *New York Times* interview that she'd once told him, "George, there was one man I wanted, and that didn't work out." When she died in 1972 at age ninety-four, Alice entrusted the petite Eden cherished by her family for nearly a century to the Preservation Society. In addition to the twelve-foot giraffe, a pair of teddy bears, and their brethren, the property features colorful annual beds, a damask rose garden, a lovely lily pond, a cutting garden, and greenhouse. A rare surviving example of a self-sustaining estate, the vegetables that earned Alice many ribbons at county fairs are harvested now for a local food bank.

The Braytons' seaside retreat may be devoid of the marble and gilt to which the owners of grander Newport mansions were accustomed, but it is notable for its collection of original interior furnishings and its second-floor display of the Preservation Society's collection of antique playthings. The house is open daily from early May through Columbus Day, but the grounds, which operate on the same schedule, are the site's chief allure. Unlike treasures sheltered within walls, the historic topiaries are fragile botanical marvels at the elements' and tourists' mercy. A 1954 hurricane dislodged the giraffe's head; in 1980, a clumsy photographer knocked off the elephant's trunk. Both took years to regrow. And unfortunately, the policeman on guard at the garden's entrance can't protect the green beasts from storms *or* stupidity: he's just a plant.

73

Part III
Massachusetts

Paul Revere House

19 North Square • Boston, MA 02113 • 617-523-2338
www.paulreverehouse.org

Henry Wadsworth Longfellow took incredible liberties when he set to verse the stirring story of *Paul Revere's Ride*. Pioneering restoration architect Joseph Everett Chandler elected a more studied approach when he was hired in 1907 to reverse two centuries of alterations and abuse endured by Boston's oldest extant residence: the Paul Revere House. The clapboard-sided, post-and-beam frame home in the North End—Boston's oldest neighborhood—was already ninety years old when Revere moved in with his elderly mother, first wife, and five children in 1770. Chandler's careful work preserved ninety percent of the original structure, built circa 1680. Dwarfed now by surrounding buildings, it alone was a bystander to Boston's seventeenth-century transition from tight-knit Puritan community to cosmopolitan seaport city.

Robert Howard, a shipping tycoon by seventeenth-century standards, was the original owner of the house, built on the site where the Second Church of Boston's parsonage stood until the building, inhabited by Increase Mather and his son, Cotton, was consumed by the Great Fire of 1676. The ample first-floor hall, a versatile space that multitasked as dining room, parlor, bedroom, workshop, and office, is furnished to reflect the period of occupancy of the wealthy merchant and his family.

Three other publicly accessible rooms are restored to their appearance during Revere's thirty-year tenure. The first-floor kitchen, with its wood-fired brick hearth, roasting reflector oven, cradle, spinning wheels, and apple slices strung across the mantel to dry, provides a glimpse of colonial women's daily lives. Revere remarried after his first wife died in 1773. Sarah and Rachel Revere each bore eight children; eleven survived. Upstairs in the best bedchamber and a second bedroom, where a few family possessions are displayed, along with a collection of pieces crafted by the accomplished silversmith, a more detailed portrait of the patriot emerges than most visitors have gleaned from poetry and history.

Revere learned his primary trade from his French Huguenot father, Apollos Rivoire, who was sent to Boston as an apprentice at age thirteen and Anglicized his name after establishing his workshop. With many mouths to feed, however, Revere also dabbled in dentistry and engraving. Regarded as a spokesperson for middle-class artisans and shopkeepers and a skilled propaganda peddler, thanks to booming sales of his colorized engraving of 1770's Boston Massacre, he became a key figure as discontent with English rule mounted. On the eve of April 18, 1775, when this leader of the Sons of Liberty set out from his petite

wooden house facing North Square on the ride that would catapult him into legend, it was not the first time he'd served as courier for the revolutionary cause, nor was he the lone rider sent to Lexington to warn Samuel Adams and John Hancock of British troop movements. Luckily for his legacy, Longfellow must have found the names William Dawes and Samuel Prescott less susceptible to rhyme.

Revere's delicately proportioned and ornately engraved silver tankards, teapots, trays, tableware, and other custom creations, as well as the more than nine hundred church bells produced by the foundry he established after the Revolution, sealed his reputation as a talented colonial craftsman. It is unlikely that his North End home, where one of twenty-three surviving Revere bells is displayed in the courtyard, would have been saved, however, had Longfellow not romanticized his midnight escapade forty-five years after Revere died at age eighty-three. Scheduled for demolition in 1902 after a century of housing a succession of first-floor shops with squalid tenement apartments above, it was purchased by Revere's great-grandson, John Phillips Reynolds, Jr., who crusaded to raise funds to rescue the abode. In 1907, the non-profit Paul Revere Memorial Association, which still operates this year-round attraction, was incorporated, and the Paul Revere House became one of America's first historic house museums when it opened to the public in 1908. While historians might decry Longfellow's embellishments, preservationists are thankful that the thousands of visitors who walk Boston's graveyard– and battleground-lined Freedom Trail each year have an opportunity to see not only how revolutionaries who risked life and livelihood for liberty died, but how they lived.

Adams National Historical Park

1250 Hancock Street • Quincy, MA 02169 • 617-770-1175
www.nps.gov/adam

Their birthplaces are side by side—two Harvard-educated lawyers, father and son, who became architects of a fledgling nation and ascended to the highest office in the land. John and John Quincy Adams—the founding father and the life-long public servant—were more worldly and well-traveled than the majority of modern Americans, yet the nation's second and sixth presidents considered only one place *home*: the once-rural Boston suburb of Quincy.

The words and ideals of these eloquent men—and their equally formidable wife and mother Abigail—still resonate, and John Adams's story remains remarkably entertaining fodder, as evinced by David McCullough's bestselling 2001 biography and the award-winning 2008 miniseries it spawned. Visitation to Adams National Historical Park surged in the wake of the book and biopic. The fourteen-acre site encompasses three historic homes—the two oldest surviving presidential birthplaces and the three-story Georgian-style Old House at Peacefield—as well as the first presidential library and a formal garden replete with a yellow-wood tree brought back from Washington, DC, by John Quincy and his mother's lilacs, roses, and sweet bay magnolia.

From mid-April through mid-November, trolleys take guests from the visitor center in downtown Quincy first to the humble seventeenth-century saltboxes—just seventy-five yards apart—where the future presidents were raised. John Adams's birthplace, constructed circa 1681 and remodeled in 1740 by

his father, farmer and shoemaker Deacon John Adams, has been restored by the park service to its appearance at the time of the American Revolution and furnished with period pieces and reproductions. Here, a portrait of the ambitious, loquacious, and contentious eldest son, who lost his first court case and vowed never again to be underprepared, emerges. Next door, inside the 1663 cottage John inherited from his father in 1761, visitors hear of the young attorney's family life, his participation in the first and second Continental Congresses, the nearly two thousand letters Abigail sent during his long absences—even though John rarely replied—and the couple's prescient decision for ten-year-old John Quincy to accompany his father to France, where the precocious boy became fluent in thirteen languages and learned

skills that would serve him well during his own diplomatic and political career.

At Peacefield, park-goers behold historic gardens and step inside the slate-roofed, wisteria-draped 1870 Stone Library, the oldest presidential repository, designed by Boston architect Edward C. Cabot and erected by John Quincy's son Charles at his father's behest. The climate-controlled library contains portraits, busts, desks belonging to both presidents, and twelve thousand volumes and documents.

The adjacent 1731 homestead, purchased and enlarged by John and Abigail in 1788 following his stint as America's first ambassador to Great Britain, remained in the Adams family until the death of great-grandson Brooks Adams in 1927. Brooks established the Adams Memorial Society to perpetuate the property and his family's

legacy. Stewardship of Peacefield was turned over to the National Park Service in 1946.

While the house reflects the occupancy of four generations, the number of artifacts from John and Abigail's era is astounding. The horseshoe Abigail hung above the entry remains, as does John's walking cane. The camelback sofa upon which the second president sat for his final portrait looks as lustrous in the Mahogany Room today as it does in Gilbert Stuart's painting. On the second floor, visitors can peer into the President's Bedroom, where a fifty-four-year love affair ended as Abigail succumbed to typhoid fever, and John opined, "I wish I could lie down beside her and die too." He could not bear to rest his head here following her death and slept instead in his study, where the secretary upon which he wrote the Treaty

of Paris ending the American Revolution and some three hundred conciliatory letters to Thomas Jefferson still occupies the northeast corner. In another corner sits the floral wing chair where the ninety-year-old Adams breathed his last words, "Thomas Jefferson survives," although the two perished just hours apart on July 4, 1826—the fiftieth anniversary of the signing of the Declaration of Independence.

Although outside the auspices of the park service, one final stop is required on an Adams immersion tour. First Parish Church, built in 1828 for a still-active congregation established in 1636, is steps from the visitor center. In addition to sitting in the Adams pew, tour participants may also descend to the crypt and stand beside the tombs of two presidents and their first ladies, whose mortal remains are forever at home.

The Wayside

455 Lexington Road • Concord, MA 01742 • 978-318-7863
www.nps.gov/mima

No small town looms larger in American legend than Concord, for not only was it the scene of the Revolutionary War's initial engagement, it was the nation's intellectual epicenter in the mid-nineteenth century, when a distinctly American brand of literature, learning, and thought was born. Just a stone's throw from the North Bridge, where the "shot heard 'round the world" was fired in 1775, sits a remarkable home that has not only witnessed some of history's most pivotal chapters but has sheltered more literary genius than any other. Of the five literary sites in the national park system, only The Wayside is associated with three notable writers.

Louisa May Alcott's teenage home was already an antique when her father, progressive educator Bronson Alcott, acquired it in 1845 with financial assistance from Concord's leading citizen—Ralph Waldo Emerson. Built circa 1686, the simple colonial farmhouse with two rooms up and two down was owned by Samuel Whitney, muster master of the Concord minutemen at the outbreak of the Battles of Lexington and Concord. Alcott added wings by lopping a barn in half. The space afforded Louisa her first private bedroom, where she jotted her earliest published works and the imaginative plays she and her three sisters staged in a barn relocated from across the street. It's now the site's visitor center. Many remembrances from her family's four-year tenure at the home they called Hillside appear in her semiautobiographical 1868 classic, *Little Women*.

In 1852, Nathaniel Hawthorne purchased the only home he ever owned from the Alcotts, rechristening it The Wayside. A year later, however, the *Scarlet Letter* and *House of Seven Gables* author was awarded an overseas diplomatic post by his college chum, newly elected President Franklin Pierce, and seven years would pass before he resettled his family in

Concord. Hawthorne made significant architectural changes to the structure, adding a second floor to the west wing and a three-story rear tower, inspired by his travels in Italy.

In 1883, Hawthorne's daughter, Rose, sold the home and many family furnishings to Boston publisher Daniel Lothrop and his wife, Harriett. The author of the *Five Little Peppers* series of children's books, under the pseudonym Margaret Sidney, was conscious of her abode's shrine-like status, and she instilled in her daughter, Margaret, born at The Wayside in 1884, a deep devotion to the property. For forty years after her mother's death, Margaret was as much curator as resident, delving into the home's history, labeling artifacts, leading tours, and ultimately ensuring its status as a National Historic Landmark. In 1965, at age eighty, she saw her birthplace safely enfolded within the boundaries of Minute Man National Historical Park.

From farmers and revolutionaries to America's first distinguished astronomer, from a fugitive slave to boarding school girls to America's fourteenth president, a pageant of humanity has slumbered beneath The Wayside's eaves; but on ranger-led tours of the centuries-old home, offered late May through late October, it is the writers who toiled here whose stories vividly emerge. While it is possible to envision the Alcott girls frolicking on the terraced lawn or Margaret Sidney dreaming up adventures for the five Pepper children in her wicker rocker, the spirit of Hawthorne most singularly imbues the home. Guests who haven't yet detected his presence can't escape it once they've ascended narrow stairs to his third-floor tower study. What was Hawthorne, already suffering the ravages of an undiagnosed condition—likely cancer—thinking when he built this "sky parlor"? Perhaps he sought refuge from sociable Bronson Alcott, who had purchased The Orchards, now also a museum, next door. Perhaps the panorama of Walden Pond sustained him. It was visible from the stand-up writing desk he used once sitting became too painful.

The unfinished novel he labored over in this elevated hideaway—discovered in a cupboard at the base of the stairs and published posthumously—may hold the answer. *Septimius Felton, or the Elixir of Life*, contains instructions for cheating death, discovered by the title character in a mysterious manuscript. Among them are the mundane: "eat no spiced meats" and "change thy shirt daily"; the virtuous: "do some decent degree of good and kindness in thy daily life" and "search not to see if thou hast a gray hair"; the cautionary: "kiss no woman if her lips be red"; and the profound: "desire nothing too fervently, not even life; yet keep thy hold upon it mightily, quietly, unshakably, for as long as thou really art resolved to live, Death, with all his force, shall have no power against thee." Scaling steep stairs and writing upright may have seemed small obstacles to the increasingly self-critical Hawthorne, who surely knew immortality lay at the tip of his pen.

William Cullen Bryant Homestead

207 Bryant Road • Cummington, MA 01026 • 413-634-2244 (seasonal) • 413-532-1631
www.thetrustees.org; Search: William Cullen Bryant Homestead

In his poem *June*, William Cullen Bryant prophetically pronounced this "flowery" month a pleasant time "to lie at rest within the ground." Flags were ordered flown at half-mast for New York City's "first citizen" when the eighty-four-year-old succumbed to a head injury in June of 1878. He had served as editor-in-chief of the *New York Evening Post* for nearly a half century, shaped Gothamites' views through thirteen presidential elections, and championed the creation of Central Park and the Metropolitan Museum of Art. His name graces midtown Manhattan's leafy oasis—Bryant Park—but while he was a New Yorker by fame and vocation, his poetry and passions had New England roots.

The verdant hills and glittering streams that provided a backdrop for youthful wanderings and inspired many melodic lines beckoned to Bryant in 1865, thirty years after his family parted with his boyhood home, built by his maternal grandfather in 1785. Although he owned a Long Island retreat in addition to his city townhouse, Bryant repurchased the farm in Cummington, Massachusetts, hoping cool country air might restore his wife's health. Frances died, however, before renovations were completed.

Although grief stricken, Bryant completed his expansion and restoration of the homestead, elevating two existing stories at the structure's southern end to add a spacious first-floor dining and entertaining area and recreating a wing the previous owner had sold to a neighbor. The space, which had been his father's medical office, became Bryant's library. Farmer and country physician Dr. Peter Bryant owned more books—seven hundred—than anyone in the area, and he encouraged his son's literary pursuits: the precocious lad published his first poem at age ten. Meanwhile, grandfather Ebenezer Snell instilled vigor in the fragile, sickly boy by engaging him in farm labor.

During summer stays at the renovated homestead and working farm, the elderly Bryant continued to exercise body and mind: a basket of dumbbells and wooden travel desk remain in his second-floor bedroom. Mary Dawes Warner, daughter of a caretaker, recalled that Bryant "never opened a gate. He would walk up to it, put his hand on it, and vault over. I have seen him at eighty years of age go over a four foot gate." And while summers were a time for recreation with visiting family and friends, Bryant reserved mornings for work, churning out editorials and the first blank verse translations of Homer's *Iliad* and *Odyssey*.

Tours of the home, which was deeded to the non-profit Trustees of Reservations in 1927 by Bryant's granddaughter, are offered Saturdays from July through Columbus Day. The interior collection of family possessions reveals much about the highly regarded man of letters, whose life coincided with America's first century and whose shoulders brushed those of many notable contemporaries. Delft tiles, Turkish lighting fixtures, and other eclectic souvenirs from Bryant's extensive travels fill the Victorian cottage.

The homestead's 195 acres are, however, where Bryant's best-known verses leap from the page. Open daily year-round, the photogenic grounds afford visitors a chance to explore the two-hundred-year-old sugar maple grove described in *Inscription for the Entrance to a Wood* or to meander a trail through an old-growth forest along the "oozy banks" immortalized in *The Rivulet* by America's first major poet. When the season he called "the year's last, loveliest smile" colors the lush landscape behind the cupolaed red barn and stalwart stone walls collect a flashy layer of tree debris, it is even possible to understand how Bryant managed to pen a significant portion of his most acclaimed poem—a meditation on death—in his teens. *Thanatopsis*, published in its final version in 1821, instructs those who fear "breathless darkness" to "Go forth, under the open sky, and list / To Nature's teachings." In autumn's gleaming transformation, limitless beauty, and gentle release, there is perennial assurance that all life is mortal yet exultant.

Hammond Castle

80 Hesperus Avenue • Gloucester, MA 01930 • 978-283-2080
www.hammondcastle.org

Inside this imposing coastal fortress, narrow stone-vaulted staircases spiral clockwise, and doors open backward—unless you're left-handed. One bedchamber appears to have no exit at all, a visual trick that unnerved unsuspecting guests. The dining room's oak wall panels are from a French monastery; its hand-painted ceiling once graced the Cordoba family's castle in Spain. Rooms and nooks are cluttered with treasures, walls draped with tapestries. A child's sarcophagus suits the décor perfectly. In the medieval village-styled courtyard, artificial rainstorms bathe lush foliage with a gentle sprinkle or a generous downpour on demand, and at the switch of a lever, the Romanesque swimming pool's thirty thousand gallons of fresh water can be exchanged for saltwater. The pool's shallow appearance is another illusion: it's actually—and luckily for the owner, who relished eliciting gasps by diving from his second-floor bedroom—eight and a half feet deep.

John Hays Hammond, Jr., was surely an imaginative kook, but visitors who stride across the drawbridge to his castle home, so audaciously out of place on the craggy shores of the working-class fishing village of Gloucester, immediately confront this reality: the man was also a genius. Mentored by family friend Thomas Edison, who introduced him to Alexander Graham Bell, Hammond devised his first invention at prep school: a door-mounted circuit breaker that enabled him to circumvent the lights-out rule. With Bell's help, the Yale graduate landed a humble clerk's post at the U.S. Patent Office. After three years, armed with insider knowledge, Hammond obtained a quarter-million-dollar loan from his father to establish the Hammond Radio Research Corporation in Gloucester in 1911. When he remotely guided a crewless yacht to Boston and back in 1914, the Navy took notice. The Father of Radio

Control went on to develop over four hundred inventions and to secure some eight hundred patents. While his work on guided torpedo systems, secret frequency radios, and other military technologies and in the fields of telephony and broadcast communications proved most lucrative, Hammond's patents were remarkably diverse: a panless stove, an electric dog, a hypodermic meat baster, luxury shaving cream, and even the concept for a home shopping network.

In another stroke of brilliance, Hammond opened his relic-filled residence and laboratory as a tax-exempt museum in 1930 and paid himself a salary as curator. Although ostensibly built as a wedding gift for his bride, Irene Fenton Reynolds, the looming structure, designed by Boston architectural firm Allen & Collens and constructed of Cape Ann granite from 1926 to 1929, indulged the inventor's enchantment with castles, sparked

by childhood years spent in England. His well-off mining engineer father dismissed Hammond's grandiose architectural fantasies as a ticket to financial ruin, but obstacles and admonishments did more to inspire than deter his ambitions.

The Great Hall, a massive high-ceilinged space straight out of the thirteenth century, houses Hammond's grandest undertaking: an organ with eighty-two hundred pipes ranging in size from four inches to thirty-two feet tall. Hammond outfitted the world's largest residential organ with a self-playing mechanism and tinkered with it for decades. It is reportedly the world's single most recorded instrument, but it is no longer playable.

Although music was one of Hammond's passions, visitors to the home he christened Abbadia Mare—Abbey-by-the-Sea—sense profound dissonance between his futuristic visions and his desire to surround himself with suits of armor, Renaissance paintings, and other artifacts. Although Irene shared his passion for collecting, it is telling that she furnished *her* bedchamber with Early American pieces. Because tours, offered mid-May through Labor Day, are self-guided, many visitors who scale Gothic tower stairs, explore labyrinthian passageways, and marvel at views overlooking Norman's Woe, the rocky reef immortalized by Longfellow in *The Wreck of the Hesperus*, leave without understanding the motives of this enigmatic innovator, who left no heirs when he died in 1965. The clue lies, perhaps, in a letter written to his father two years before undertaking the project. "After I am gone, all my scientific creations will be old fashioned and forgotten," Hammond lamented, already cognizant of progress's pace. "I want to build something in hard stone and engrave on it for posterity a name of which I am justly proud."

Historic Deerfield

80 Old Main Street • Deerfield, MA 01342 • 413-775-7214

www.historic-deerfield.org

"I left Deerfield wishing that there was a 'Mrs. Flynt' in every community across the land," Lady Bird Johnson wrote to her hostess following a 1973 visit to the Massachusetts town Helen and Henry Flynt had transformed into a museum of early New England life. The Flynts didn't intend to create a miniature Colonial Williamsburg, but as often happens with collectors—especially those of means—the purchase, restoration, and decoration of one colonial home in 1945 sparked further acquisitions. The Flynts bought hoards of antiques and property after property, demolishing or relocating structures that didn't fit on The Street and restoring those that did. Although locals raised eyebrows and modern preservationists frown on the romanticization that characterized Colonial Revival mentality, the couple's legacy is a mile-long expanse widely considered to be New England's loveliest thoroughfare.

Visitors who immerse themselves in the Historic Deerfield experience come to understand that life in this northwesternmost English settlement was anything but quaint. The frontier outpost was incessantly attacked by the French and their native allies from its permanent establishment in 1682 until the late 1720s. The 1704 Raid during Queen Anne's War decimated Deerfield: more than half the population was taken captive or killed. The eleven historic house museums in Historic Deerfield's collection, open mid-April through late November, date from the 1730s through the 1840s—a period of peace and prosperity for the town's farmers and tradespeople. By 1936, when the Flynts enrolled their son at the Deerfield Academy, a preparatory school founded in 1797, many of these architectural treasures were in sorry shape after a century of economic decline, during which Deerfielders developed cottage crafts industries to sustain themselves.

Each house is a page in Deerfield's plotline with a subplot all its own. The powder-blue clapboard Wells-Thorn House is a good starting point: Each room is themed to represent a different year, from the 1725 entry to the 1850 attic teeming with a century's castoffs. The circa 1750 Frary House was restored in the 1890s by historian C. Alice Baker, long before the Flynts arrived on the scene, and contains examples of local Arts and Crafts period handiwork. An adult-sized cradle at the Sheldon House, a mid-1750s duplex that sheltered a middle-class farming family, is a poignant remnant from the first quarter of the nineteenth century, when tuberculosis was New England's leading cause of death. The Federal-style brick Stebbins House dates to 1799; its Neoclassical interior befits the Deerfield Academy benefactor's status as one of the town's wealthiest land and business owners.

By special arrangement, visitors can even tour the Flynts' Deerfield residence, bequeathed following Helen's death in 1986 to the non-profit they founded in 1952. The 1734 Allen House was the pair's first project, and it remains exactly as they left it—overcoats slung casually over chairs in their parlor-bedroom, fine paintings and needlecraft on the walls, meticulously selected antiques everywhere.

The Ashley House, built in 1734 for Jonathan Ashley, likewise overflows with more colonial paraphernalia than the settlement's second pastor could have imagined possessing. Additional furnishings and textiles amassed by the founders, who competed with the Rockefellers, Du Ponts, and other elite collectors, are on view inside the Flynt Center of Early New England Life, making Historic Deerfield one of America's foremost repositories of colonial decorative arts. As is the case at most museums, you're not allowed to touch these exquisite pieces, but you may be touched by them as you contemplate the pride with which they were crafted, the faith and perseverance of those who utilized them, and even the humor that transcends centuries. Six glazed English earthenware plates on a cupboard shelf in the Ashley House impart timeless truth:

What is a merrey man?
Let him doe what he cane
to entertain his guests
with wine and merrey jests;
But if his wife doth frowne
all merriment goes downe.

And while handling objects is verboten, you may trod upon Historic Deerfield's oldest artifact. The Street itself—laid out by English surveyors in the 1670s—traces a path blazed by the native Pocumtucks.

Chesterwood

4 Williamsville Road • Stockbridge, MA 01262 • 413-298-3579
www.chesterwood.org

On April 19, 1875—one hundred years to the day after the first blood was spilled in America's campaign for independence—commemorative exercises in Concord, Massachusetts, featured the debut of a life-sized bronze statue of a resolute young farmer-soldier. Dignitaries present at the *Minute Man*'s unveiling included President Grant, Henry Wadsworth Longfellow, and Ralph Waldo Emerson—who had lobbied fellow monument committee members to award the statue's commission to an untested local. Conspicuously absent from the dedication of one of his most famous works was the twenty-four-year-old sculptor himself, Daniel Chester French. The MIT dropout was in Florence, honing his newfound talent.

Throughout his prolific, illustrious, and lucrative career, French, who was legendary for on-time delivery, took the sculpting business seriously. When he returned from Italy in 1876, his father, Henry Flagg French—a lawyer and farmer who invented the French drain and served as first president of Massachusetts Agricultural College before being named assistant secretary of the treasury—helped him to win several commissions in Washington, DC. Within ten years of establishing a studio in his boyhood home of Concord in 1879, French had emerged as one of

the American Renaissance's leading artists.

By 1896, with his primary studio now located in New York City, French possessed both the means and the desire to acquire a country place, and he set about transforming a scruffy Stockbridge farm—with incredible views of Monument Mountain—into a true artist's retreat. French hired long-time friend and sometime collaborator architect Henry Bacon to design a modern home and gracious and spacious studio reminiscent of an Italian villa. French undertook the plan for the gardens and grounds, seeking to marry the setting with the structures and proving as able a landscape architect as he was a sculptor.

Chesterwood now welcomes visitors daily late May through mid-October, the same months French, his wife, Mary, and their daughter, Margaret, escaped to the Berkshires each year. House tours are limited to first-floor rooms, including the parlor, study, and dining room—all decorated with original art and furnishings. French's genius, however, is best understood by walking the property, which reflects his keen sense of proportion, scale, detail, and geometric form, and by viewing exhibits in the Barn Gallery and studio, where the diligent artist reported to work at 9:00 a.m. six mornings each week.

Peer inside the studio from the sprawling piazza, where the Frenches entertained neighbors from all walks during Friday afternoon open houses, and you'll immediately see an immense—yet small by comparison to the nineteen-foot final version—plaster cast of the most recognizable of French's more than one hundred monuments. The seated Lincoln, housed within the Doric-columned Lincoln Memorial designed by

Bacon for the nation's capital, was the artist's most intense assignment. Charged with capturing the president as preserver of the Union, French spent three years refining and scaling up the clay model he presented to the National Commission on Fine Arts in 1914. Then, it took the Bronx-based Piccirilli Brothers eight years to carve the figure in twenty-eight marble pieces. Although the memorial was dedicated in 1922, French—whose Stockbridge studio had a rail system that allowed him to wheel hefty pieces out into the sunlight—did not consider it complete until 1927, when lighting was installed to compensate for murky shadows cast by the reflecting pool.

Photos of French unwinding in his studio garden depict a man seemingly pleased with his environs. Modeled after an Italian Renaissance garden—only with a season-spanning profusion of colorful blossoms to please his wife—the layout incorporated careful plantings, architectural features created by the artist, and fruit trees original to the property, which continued to operate as a gentleman's farm. French also added woodland pathways, and the Glade—a circular clearing with a contoured, narrowing stairway entering the forest—shows off his well-developed sense of perspective.

In 1906, French noted, "Our place comes more into shape as the years roll off and looks most too fine for a mere artist now." Through the efforts of the National Trust for Historic Preservation, to which Margaret, a sculptor like her father, transferred Chesterwood in 1968, French's home now inspires myriad artists and provides a fitting setting for an outdoor installation of contemporary works of sculpture each summer.

The Mount

2 Plunkett Street • Lenox, MA 01240 • 413-551-5111
www.edithwharton.org

Fewer than five percent of National Historic Landmarks focus on women; sites that exude a woman's influence are rarer still. The Mount was not only Edith Wharton's home from 1902 until 1911 and birthplace of her finest novels, but it was the manifestation of the design sensibilities she espoused in her first book, *The Decoration of Houses*. Cowritten with Ogden Codman, Jr., and published in 1897, this groundbreaking treatise on interior spaces railed against Victorian excesses and advocated classic European ideals of symmetry, balance, proportion, and harmony with nature.

Although the self-educated Wharton, who churned out more than forty books during a forty-year span, was best known for novels like the scandalous 1905 bestseller *The House of Mirth* and 1920's *The Age of Innocence*, for which she was the first woman awarded a Pulitzer Prize for fiction, she considered landscape gardening her chief talent. From the moment visitors begin the quarter-mile stroll along the maple-lined drive Wharton designed with input from her niece, renowned landscape architect Beatrix Farrand, they are immersed in her aesthetic principals. Although Codman and architect Francis L.V. Hoppin contributed to the plans for the classical revival–style country house, and Farrand fashioned the kitchen garden, the estate's every detail embodied Wharton's vision.

Wharton spent the pinnacle years of her career in Lenox, entertaining literary friends like Henry James, who provided the encouragement she was denied as a child. Wharton began telling stories before she could read. When her mother refused to supply paper, she jotted poems and tales on salvaged brown parcel wrappings. Married off at twenty-three to Teddy Wharton, who was twelve years older, unemployed, bipolar, and a philanderer, she was sustained emotionally by her writing and financially by an inheritance from a distant relative

until her success surged. Her own disastrous affair and Teddy's deteriorating condition likely led her to flee for France in 1911; their divorce was finalized in 1913.

The Mount had a succession of private owners, housed a girls' boarding school from 1942 until 1976, and was leased for performances by Shakespeare & Company from 1978 until 2001, even as the edifice crumbled and its formal gardens vanished beneath the overgrowth. Edith Wharton Restoration, a non-profit formed in 1980 to acquire the house and nearly fifty of the estate's original 128 acres, began costly restoration work in 1997, but drama unfolded over the Shakespearean troupe's ouster and the threat of foreclosure, which remains a serious challenge to the overextended organization.

Tours of The Mount, offered daily early May through October, reveal a restoration that is very much a work in progress. Although the building has been extensively renovated inside and out, and main floor rooms showcase decorators' interpretations

of Wharton's design dictates installed in 2002, few original possessions remain. A notable exception—a collection of Wharton's books acquired at great cost in 2006 and returned to the home after more than a century in Europe—is on view in the library. However, the second-floor chamber where she spent each morning writing in bed, scattering the pages of works such as *Ethan Frome* on the floor for her secretary to retrieve and transcribe, is devoid of furnishings.

"No one fully knows our Edith who hasn't seen her in the act of creating a habitation for herself," her friend James once

remarked, and The Mount's survival is critical to future understanding of this multifaceted woman, whose stories chronicled the demise of the American high society into which she was born. Wharton believed a home's most elegant face should be hidden from strangers, but it would be tragic for the public to lose access to the gardens that were her consummate achievement. Carefully reconstructed based upon photographs, letters, and garden forensics at a cost of three million dollars, the Italianate hidden garden and formal French-style flower garden, with its dolphin fountain and three thousand blooming annuals and perennials, were laid out by Wharton to provide a gracious and gradual transition between her home and the distant lake and wilds. "This place, every line of which is my own work," she wrote in 1911 before bidding The Mount adieu, "far surpasses *The House of Mirth.*"

Naumkeag

5 Prospect Hill Road • Stockbridge, MA 01262 • 413-298-3239
www.thetrustees.org; Search: Naumkeag

Stanford White, of famed architectural firm McKim, Mead and White, designed many of the Gilded Age's most splendid residences, including Naumkeag, named for the native word for Salem, Massachusetts—the birthplace of owner and eminent Manhattan attorney Joseph Hodges Choate. The forty-four room summer cottage in the bucolic Berkshires, completed in 1886, sports an imposing brick-and-stone towered entrance and a rustic wood-shingled rear façade with decorative patinated copper gutters and sparkles of green glass in the window mortar. The comparably detailed interior features White's signature arched doorways and recessed nooks; rich mahogany, cherry, and oak paneling and moldings; and a hand-carved three-flight oak staircase that mimics the graceful curvature of the mountains outside.

It is not, however, the architecture—nor the American, European, and Asian furniture, art, and ceramics amassed during the Choate family's travels—that makes Naumkeag a jewel. In what may have been subconscious one-upsmanship, Fletcher Steele bested White in his elaborate and imaginative treatment of the mansion's environs.

Steele met Naumkeag's second-generation owner, Mabel Choate, at a Lenox Garden Club meeting in 1926, sparking a thirty-year friendship and collaborative effort to transform the estate. Steele, who dropped out of Harvard's new landscape architecture program in 1908, created more than seven hundred gardens: Naumkeag—his most ambitious commission—is one of only two publicly accessible survivors. Thanks to Mabel's enthusiasm and means, Naumkeag became an experimental playground for the father of modern landscape design. When Mabel asked Steele to add steps leading down a steep bank to her cutting garden, "little did I realize what I was in for," she recalled. The Blue Steps are both practical and breathtaking. Each step is a different height and requires varied exertion, which makes the descent

nearly effortless. Gazing back uphill, the Italianate- and Art Deco-inspired stairway, with its white pipe railings, trickling water, and vivid arcs of blue, rises ethereally amid a throng of paper birches. Steele, who tested several colors before settling on the azure hue, described his crowning achievement as "a hint of movement, of grace promised, of beauty that hides or lies forgotten."

From his first project—the Afternoon Garden—to the culminating Chinese Garden with its brick walls, temple, and Moon Gate, Steele created a series of outdoor rooms carefully sited within the sloping property to take advantage of surrounding views. The Afternoon Garden, for example, is delineated by pilings dredged up from Boston Harbor and topped with ornate Venetian-inspired capitals: each pair frames discrete scenes of lush foliage and rounded peaks. Steele was also mindful of the aerial

appearance of his garden compartments: the rose garden, with its undulating walkways, was specifically designed to be viewed from Mabel's second-floor bedroom.

At Steele's urging, Mabel, who never married, bequeathed Naumkeag and its forty-eight acres of gardens, farmland, and woodland to the Trustees of Reservations with instructions that her home remain exactly as she left it during her final summer stay in 1958. That means a dog bed still sits in the dining room, where President William McKinley asked her father to serve as ambassador to England. A linen closet brims with Mabel's monogrammed towels. A 1958 train schedule hangs on the pantry wall. And visitors see not only impressive artifacts like John Singer Sargent charcoal portraits, a Flemish tapestry, and antiques Mabel's mother, Caroline, selected with White's advice on New York City sprees, but also mundane objects stowed

in closets: umbrellas, coats, golf clubs, a vacuum cleaner.

Weather and nature's whimsy necessitate more active intervention when it comes to landscape preservation, but the Trustees of Reservations, a privately supported organization with a venerable record of saving Massachusetts properties, can rely on detailed plans and mounds of correspondence between Choate and Steele for guidance. The organization offers house and garden tours daily between Memorial Day and Columbus Day weekends. Most visitors can't resist a stroll past the three-hundred-year-old oak that shaded the Choates' earliest picnics to the South Lawn's cast-iron pagoda, not because of the photogenic Japanese maples that surround it but due to the rumored powers of the sacred rock enshrined inside on a Ming pedestal. Whether or not rubbing this souvenir from Mabel's 1935 visit to Beijing's Summer Palace improves your memory, Naumkeag isn't a place you'll soon forget.

Part IV

Vermont

Park-McCullough House

1 Park Street • North Bennington, VT 05257 • 802-442-5441
www.parkmccullough.org

In 1865, gold rush millionaire Trenor Park built an exceptional Victorian villa in the unlikeliest of places: rural southwestern Vermont. The fashionable thirty-five-room three-story house was a manifestation of this enterprising Vermonter's attainment of the American Dream. The son of a humble lumberman, Park passed the bar exam at twenty-one without ever attending law school. In 1852, he and his wife, Laura, and daughter, Lizzie, set out for California on the heels of his father-in-law, Hiland Hall, who had been appointed to a federal commission charged with settling the myriad land claims that arose following the discovery of gold. Within eleven years, Park had amassed a fortune through his legal practice and management of John C. Frémont's Mariposa mines.

Capitulating to Laura's longing to return to New England, Park purchased two hundred acres of farmland from her father and channeled his energies into the construction of a gracious manor–inspired home incorporating the latest advances. England–born New York -based architect Henry

Dudley, known for his Gothic churches, was hired to design the contemporary Second Empire-style house, with its characteristic slate-shingled bell-cast mansard roof and rectangular tower. Even a miniature replica that served initially as a doghouse was constructed on-site. It was later converted to a children's playhouse, complete with scale furnishings and a working cast-iron stove. The Parks moved in on Christmas Day, and although they occupied the home only during the winter holidays and summer season, it had every comfort: spacious closets, a rising hot air heating system, hot running water—even on the second floor—and a basement gas machine that illuminated an impressive collection of gasoliers.

The first floor's high-ceilinged seventy-five-foot center hall, library, music room, billiard room, and dining room served as sumptuous yet comfortable gathering spaces for visitors who called upon the family, whose prominence in Vermont was cemented when Hall was elected governor in 1858. Lizzie, whose husband John McCullough also served a term as Vermont's governor from 1902 to 1904, bought out her siblings following her father's death and continued to summer in North Bennington until she died at age ninety in 1938. Lizzie and John's daughter, Bess, lived in the home until her death in 1965—a century after its intricate cast plaster ceilings, marble fireplaces, and radiant woodwork first were unveiled.

The family did little to alter the home during this hundred-year span, and they never discarded anything, leaving researchers with a trove of receipts, construction and maintenance records, photographs, menus—even Lizzie's gowns and love letters. Wallcoverings and textiles are in remarkably fine condition. The Otis elevator, installed in the 1930s for aging Lizzie, remains in working order.

The interior was renovated only once, in 1891, when the McCulloughs hosted President Benjamin Harrison, who spoke at the dedication of the Bennington Battle Monument in Vermont's centennial year. As any hostess might, Lizzie flew into action in the months preceding the president's arrival: The center hall received a Colonial Revival makeover, complete with parquet floors and an inglenook; the dining room was enlarged to accommodate a massive Italian Renaissance–style table brought up from the McCulloughs' New York City residence.

The estate's grounds, which once encompassed six hundred acres, have been altered. Gardens, including picturesque rose beds, have been relocated to the rear of the structure, and the refurbished carriage barn is used as a special events venue. But as guests step inside the Victorian mansion from the sweeping verandah, they enter a space essentially unaltered since Harrison enjoyed two nine-course feasts in the dining room and climbed the grand staircase, with its oak-columned landing and Tiffanyesque skylight, to sleep in

131

Lizzie's bedroom: an occurrence that would have undoubtedly delighted Trenor Park.

Shortly after inheriting his great-grandfather's estate, John McCullough II founded the non-profit Park-McCullough House Association, which offers daily tours mid-May through mid-October of this rare reminder of an era when a vein of precious metal sparked a new American belief that anyone with ambition, moxie, and a touch of luck just might strike gold and alter his destiny.

Hildene

1005 Hildene Road • Manchester, VT 05254 • 802-362-1788 • 800-578-1788
www.hildene.org

Abraham Lincoln never set foot in Vermont, yet his legacy is singularly preserved in the picturesque Battenkill Valley town of Manchester. Always a popular figure in the state, the sixteenth president commanded three-quarters of Vermonters' votes in 1860 and 1864, but his post-Civil War plans to vacation at Manchester's Equinox Hotel in 1865—as his wife, Mary Todd, and sons Robert and Tad had the previous two summers—were thwarted by an assassin's bullet. Why, then, is this Manchester home to a remarkable collection of Lincoln family possessions, including one of only three surviving stovepipe hats worn by the president?

When Robert Todd Lincoln, whose fortunes were as exalted as his father's origins were humble, deigned to purchase a country estate, his thoughts turned to the mountain-sheltered Vermont town he'd known in his youth. The Harvard-educated attorney, businessman, and diplomat—whose three brothers perished before reaching adulthood—purchased five hundred acres in 1902. Three years later, he and his wife took up summer residence at Hildene, the eight-thousand-square-foot twenty-four-room Georgian Revival mansion designed by the Boston firm of Shepley, Rutan & Coolidge. For seven decades, the gracious farm estate was inhabited by Lincoln descendants, who added personal touches while protecting possessions and perpetuating family legends.

Many of the home's furnishings have fascinating stories. The rare player pipe-organ, installed at a cost equivalent to five million dollars today, was an anniversary gift to Robert's wife, Mary Harlan Lincoln, along with 242 music rolls. When the organ was restored in 1980 after forty years of silence, these rolls were digitized. Now, they're safely stored, while the pipes still intone tunes from yesteryear. In the parlor, a large bookcase bears the name

of Chicago's Marshall Field's Department Store. Robert was devastated in 1906 when his friend, Field, died of pneumonia two weeks after the two painted golf balls pink for an ill-fated round of New Year's Day play in the snow.

In Robert's library office, the ruby walls, tufted sofa, and floor-skimming drapes are reminiscent of a luxurious Pullman train car, which is not surprising, since the president's son was named the Pullman Company's president in 1898 and served as chairman until his death at Hildene in 1926. A letterpress—precursor to modern photocopiers—saw heavy use in the office: twenty

thousand documents were discovered here. The fireplace, according to tales, is where some of Abraham Lincoln's private papers were destroyed before Robert finally relinquished to the Library of Congress, in 1919, the eight trunkloads of documents he'd removed from the White House.

Hildene remained a summer residence for Robert's wife and eldest daughter, Mamie, but following their deaths, Mary "Peggy" Lincoln Beckwith, the president's great-granddaughter, made the farm her full-time home. Peggy inherited a wild streak from her oft-married mother, Jessie—the youngest of Robert and Mary's three children. Peggy flew airplanes, drove fast cars, and invited animals—as many as eighteen dogs, cats, and raccoons—into the mansion. Like her grandfather, who would only appear on his late father's behalf if not required to speak, she was somewhat burdened by her ancestry. Peggy never married. Her brother Bud did—thrice—but had no children. So, the Lincoln line ended when he died in 1985.

When the Christian Science Church found it impossible to maintain the property bequeathed to them by Peggy in 1975, the Friends of Hildene, now three hundred volunteers strong, sprang up to save and showcase this treasure. The non-profit offers a year-round schedule of daily tours and special programs and maintains Hildene's 412 acres of gardens and farmland. Snowshoers and cross-country skiers enjoy the estate's trails each winter. In spring, the formal English garden, designed by Jessie as a gift for her mother in 1907, begins to bloom. Its hedges and beds are arranged to resemble a stained glass window. Visitors enjoy hayrides to the farm through the summer months and spectacular views of the Green and Taconic mountains' mottled hues come autumn. It's easy to imagine the Great Emancipator tipping his tall black hat, part of an impressive collection of presidential memorabilia displayed in Robert Todd Lincoln's original upstairs bedroom, to this harmonious scene.

President Calvin Coolidge State Historic Site

3780 Route 100A • Plymouth Notch, VT 05056 • 802-672-3773
www.historicvermont.org/coolidge

America's thirtieth president was a small town boy. The Vermont village where Calvin Coolidge was born on the Fourth of July in 1872 was so tiny, in fact, that when the Plymouth Old-Time Dance Orchestra visited the White House, a *New York Times* headline proclaimed, "Half of His Native Village Makes a Call on the President." Since only twenty-nine souls inhabited Plymouth Notch in 1926, this was no exaggeration. Neither is it a stretch to declare the Calvin Coolidge State Historic Site the nation's preeminent presidential birthplace. The entire village, little altered since the early twentieth century, is a National Historic Landmark, preserved in honor of the humble son who took the nation's helm here in the Vermont hills.

Attached to the general store that his father ran, and later owned, is the diminutive home where the president was born,

complete with original furnishings and family possessions. Next door, the 1840 Greek Revival–style Union Christian Church displays an American flag aside the president's pew. The post and beam Wilder Barn, built circa 1875, houses antique agricultural implements; the adjacent horse barn, meticulously reconstructed in 2003, showcases a fine array of horse-drawn sleighs, carriages, and coaches. The Wilder House, built as a tavern in 1830, is once again a restaurant; in 1868, it was the setting for the wedding of the president's parents.

Calvin's father, Colonel John Coolidge, was one of the original investors in the Plymouth Cheese Factory up the hill. Operated by the president's son, John, until 1998, when it was acquired by the state, it is leased to Plymouth Artisan Cheese, which still sells the tangy and moist, curd-style cheese for which the Coolidge family was known. The cheese-making process can often be observed, and the original 1890 equipment is displayed on the factory's second floor.

Most fascinating, however, is the Coolidge Homestead—the simple abode the family purchased when Cal was four. From

the eat-in-kitchen with its table set for four to the two-hole privy, the home appears quite exactly as it did in 1923, when Vice President Coolidge vacationed here. On August 3 of that year, Calvin and his wife, Grace, were awakened by the colonel, who, as a notary, could administer the presidential oath to his son. In the parlor, now christened the Oath of Office Room, the family Bible, kerosene lamp, and pearl-handled pen are arranged on a table just as they were at 2:47 a.m. that morning, when Calvin swore to defend the Constitution following Warren G. Harding's assassination. "It seemed a simple and natural thing to do at the time," the president reflects in his autobiography.

Plymouth Notch's place in history was already cemented, but in 1924, the nation's attention turned again to the terse, sharp-witted, outdoorsy president's hometown when he set up his summer White House there following the distressing death of his sixteen-year-old younger son. The press, curious tourists, and luminaries like Henry Ford, Thomas Edison, and Harvey and Russell Firestone flocked to Vermont. Clippings in Coolidge Hall, the dance hall above the general-store-turned-office for the commander in chief and his staff, tell of the hoopla. The president's presence had perhaps the most profound effect on Plymouth's postmaster, who was paid based on postage revenues. What was normally a fifty-dollar-per-year job netted fifteen hundred dollars that summer.

Plymouth Notch Cemetery, located across Route 100A, is the final resting place for six generations of Coolidges, including the president. From late May to mid-October annually, however, Silent Cal's legacy comes to life in Plymouth Notch. Visitor Center exhibits tell the story of an effective president, who restored integrity to the office following Harding's scandal-marred tenure; drastically reduced government spending, the national debt, and income taxes; and delivered the first presidential radio address. As visitors stroll picturesque lanes, sip cold Moxie on the general store's porch, and immerse themselves in the life of a man who never forgot his heritage, they can't help but sense the self-reliant, down-to-earth values that inspired Coolidge to tell a Bennington audience in 1928: "If the spirit of liberty should vanish in other parts of the Union, and support of our institutions should languish, it could all be replenished from the generous store held by the people of this brave little state of Vermont."

Morrill Homestead

Justin Smith Morrill Highway • Strafford, VT 05072
802-765-4484 (seasonal) • 802-828-3051
www.historicvermont.org/morrill

As historic figures go, Justin Smith Morrill isn't exactly a household name. His chief legacy, the Land-Grant Act of 1862, might not ring bells either. Yet by sponsoring this federal legislation, Morrill was, in many ways, the architect of the American Dream.

Born the son of a blacksmith in Strafford, Vermont, in 1810, the studious lad dreamed of attending college, but practicality led him to take a job as store clerk in the village at age fifteen. Two years later, Morrill founded a subscription library in town, selling shares for two dollars each. Hard-working, shrewd, and ambitious, yet respected for his honesty, common sense, and altruism, Morrill proved a successful businessman. With his mentor and partner, Judge Jedediah Harris, he eventually owned and operated four general stores, and by the age of thirty-eight, he'd amassed sufficient wealth to purchase a fifty-acre plot and retire to a life as a gentleman farmer.

In designing his country estate, the self-made Vermonter turned, of course, to books. None were more influential than the opinionated treatises of Andrew Jackson Downing, the mid-nineteenth century's leading arbiter of landscape design and architectural style. Morrill's plans for his seventeen-room Gothic Revival cottage—with its steeply pitched finial-topped roofs, embellished window moldings, and elaborately carved bargeboards dripping delicately from the eaves—took to heart Downing's teachings. Most notably, Morrill heeded Downing's counsel to "look to nature for hints in color." He painted his home a pale sandy shade when it was completed in 1851, then a livelier, rosier hue following the Civil War. Both would have pleased Downing, who advised in *The Architecture of Country Houses* that white "is too glaring and conspicuous. It is absolutely painful."

Just as Morrill turned his attention to raising a family and designing his gardens and experimental farm, his brief retirement came to an end. In characteristic fashion, when

approached in 1854 to run for the U.S. House of Representatives, Morrill carefully studied his chances of being elected before throwing his hat into the ring. During an accomplished congressional career, first in the House, then as senator from Vermont from 1867 until his death in 1898, Morrill's self-acquired knowledge served him well. He chaired the Public Buildings and Grounds Committee during a period when many landmarks, including the Library of Congress, were constructed and helped shore up the nation's currency as chairman of the Senate Finance Committee during the critical time following the Civil War. Morrill showed greatest foresight, however, in his dogged pursuit of the passage of the Land-Grant Act, which he authored in 1857 and advocated until it was signed into law by Abraham

Lincoln in 1862. The Morrill Act revolutionized higher education by funneling funds generated through the sale of federal lands to the endowment of public colleges and universities—at least one per state—where students from working-class backgrounds could study not only the classics but agriculture, mechanical sciences, and other practical professions.

The more than one hundred colleges that trace their origins to the Land-Grant Act have offered immeasurable opportunity to millions, including many graduates from humble backgrounds. The Morrill Homestead in rural Strafford celebrates the role this native son played in fostering Americans' cherished belief in universal potential. During his forty-four years in Washington, DC, Morrill continued to summer at the pink cottage, which remained in his family until 1938. In 1960, his home was designated Vermont's first National Historic Landmark. In 1969, it became a state historic site.

On weekends from Memorial Day through Columbus Day, visitors can amble through the gardens, recreated from Morrill's detailed notes and sketches; explore farm buildings, including the exhibit-filled coach house and petite, Gothic-detailed ice house; and tour the mansion, eclectically furnished with a combination of original Victorian antiques, collected items, and pieces from the senator's Washington home. The dim and intimate library, with its stained glass windows and skylight, displays Morrill's most prized possessions. It was these volumes that fill the floor-to-ceiling bookcases, after all, that transformed a country storekeeper and farmer into a visionary statesman.

Marsh-Billings-Rockefeller National Historical Park

Vermont Route 12 • Woodstock, VT 05091 • 802-457-3368

www.nps.gov/mabi

The fifteen-thousand-square-foot Queen Anne–style brick mansion with a billionaire's view of Woodstock's lush and curvaceous landscape was deemed a National Historic Landmark three decades before it became the centerpiece of Vermont's first national park. Tucked within one of America's oldest sustainably managed forests, the structure that sheltered a succession of prescient environmentalists helps to tell the larger story of emerging consciousness of humans' impact on their natural surroundings. The former estate of Laurance and Mary Rockefeller, crisscrossed by twenty miles of carriage roads on five hundred and fifty sloping acres on Mount Tom, became the first conservation-themed national park when it debuted in 1998. Named for its three principal owners, the site, unlike many suspended-in-time historic properties, interprets a two-century period of land stewardship.

George Perkins Marsh, the park's first namesake, was born in Woodstock in 1801 and grew up in the property's original Federal-style house, built by his father, Charles, in 1805. His parents had to curtail the inquisitive boy's reading by the time he was eight to protect his faltering eyesight. Forced to spend time outdoors, he observed the transformation taking place as the Green Mountain State's dense woods were harvested for timber and clear-cut for farming. A perpetual scholar, Marsh became an attorney, a linguist proficient in twenty languages, a farmer, businessman, and eventually—like his father—a congressman. In 1864, while serving as the United States' first minister to the kingdom of Italy, Marsh's dismay at the devastation wrought by overfarming the Mediterranean hillsides, combined with his Vermont recollections, inspired *Man and Nature*, a cautionary text with the stated objective of indicating "the character and, approximately, the extent of the changes produced by

human action in the physical conditions of the globe we inhabit."

Unlike Marsh's previously published books about Icelandic grammar and camels, this seminal work ensured his legacy as a founder of the conservation movement. A copy of *Man and Nature*, marked up by Frederick Billings, was discovered in the Marsh-Billings-Rockefeller home's library. Billings, another self-made Vermonter, went west in 1848, not to seek gold, but to hang out his shingle in San Francisco, where his land claims practice thrived. Billings served as California attorney general and named the town and college of Berkeley before returning in 1861 to the East Coast. He met Julia Parmly in New York City, married her within four weeks, and, in 1869, purchased the Marsh farm for his expanding family.

History might not view Billings, for whom Montana's largest city is named, as an impeccable environmentalist: He was, after all, one of the original investors in and short-term president of the transcontinental Northern Pacific Railroad, which displaced native tribes and animal herds. He did, however, take Marsh's prophesies to heart and was a crusader for reforestation, a patron of artists whose works stirred desire to protect American landscapes, and a progressive dairy farmer emulated for his innovative practices.

Billings refashioned his Woodstock abode in Victorian Stick style in 1869, then again in 1885 in the newly popular Queen Anne style. Architect Henry Hudson Holly's remodel added ornamental brickwork outside and Tiffany wallpapers, fabrics, and stained glass windows inside. The rural residence

was inherited by Billings's granddaughter, Mary French Rockefeller, in 1954. While the Rockefellers' updates included gardens, tennis courts, and a swimming pool, they used the home only six weeks each summer, and Mary refurbished many family possessions, exhibiting surprising New England thriftiness for a woman of means. In 1983, the couple established the Woodstock Foundation to operate Billings Farm, located across the street, as a living agrarian museum. Five years before Mary's death in 1997, she and Laurance, a philanthropist and conservationist who served as environmental adviser to five presidents, bequeathed the remainder of the estate to the American people with strict instructions for its preservation.

Ranger-led mansion tours, offered late May through October, highlight interior details and striking collections. Each first-floor room's paneling is made from a different wood; each parquet floor has a unique design. Victorian furnishings remain, as do modern artifacts and family photos. The home's most notable—and valuable—collection is its art, including two dozen Hudson River School paintings. An Albert Bierstadt canvas, which would be any other home's most prized possession, hangs casually above knick-knack-strewn shelves, and a Niagara Falls scene painted in 1830 by the school's founder graces the entryway. Founder Thomas Cole displayed radical environmental ideas thirty-four years before Marsh's treatise, it seems. The miniscule figure gesturing toward the mighty falls surely symbolizes humans' insignificance in nature's grand scheme.

Part V
New Hampshire

PIERCE HOMESTEAD

The Pierce Homestead was built in 1804 by Benjamin Pierce, a general in the American Revolution, twice governor of New Hampshire (1827-28, 1829-30), and father of Franklin Pierce, the 14th President of the United States (1853-57). Franklin Pierce was born in Hillsboro November 23, 1804 and the family occupied this dwelling shortly thereafter.

Franklin Pierce Homestead

301 2nd NH Turnpike • Hillsborough, NH 03244 • 603-478-3165
www.nhstateparks.org; Search: Franklin Pierce Homestead State Historic Site

Scholarly rankings and popular opinion both dub Franklin Pierce one of the poorest performing presidents in U.S. history. Not surprisingly, the only president to hail from New Hampshire is a more sympathetic figure in his native Hillsborough. A visit to the boyhood home of the fourteenth president not only provides a glimpse of the lifestyle enjoyed by a prominent family at the outset of the nineteenth century—it also reveals the reluctance and heavy heart with which Pierce took the oath of office.

Benjamin Pierce built the two-story wood-frame home in 1804, the same year Franklin, the seventh of his eight children, was born. The elder Pierce, a distinguished Revolutionary War veteran, blazed a political trail his son would follow. Initially, Benjamin operated a tavern, and, as brigadier general of the state militia, held drills in the second-floor ballroom, which runs the length of the building. As this self-made man's fortunes and influence grew, his fine residence in rural Hillsborough remained a gathering place for the community and visiting notables like Daniel Webster and Nathaniel Hawthorne—Franklin's Bowdoin College classmate. In 1827, the year his father was elected to the first of two stints as governor, Franklin established his law practice across the street. He finally moved out of his parents' abode—to a place down the road—after marrying Jane Means Appleton four days before his thirtieth birthday.

Tours of the homestead, which is restored to its circa 1824 appearance, highlight Pierce family possessions, displayed alongside other period and reproduction pieces. The sideboard in the tavern room was a wedding gift to Franklin and his bride. Jane's piano occupies a corner of the sitting room, which was wallpapered with scenes of the Bay of Naples in 1824. Hand-stenciled wall embellishments, such as the ballroom's candle with holly-and-pine design

commemorating Benjamin's Christmas birthday, have been painstakingly recreated. The ballroom's springy floorboards evoke the lively dances held here, but the artifacts and news clippings displayed on a long curved table that occupied the state senate chamber in Concord during Franklin Pierce's tenure as speaker shed light on the personal tragedies that contributed to his ineffectual presidency.

History remembers Pierce as the only sitting president ever denied renomination by his party, a chief executive whose policies fostered divisiveness and failed to prevent the young nation his father fought to establish from hurtling toward Civil War. In Hillsborough, however, Pierce emerges as a more complex character, whose ascendancy to the presidency was something of a fluke and whose political ambitions were always at odds with the desires of his fragile, reticent wife, who convinced him to resign his senate seat in 1842 after a decade in congress. Franklin returned to practicing law in

Concord, turning down political appointments. When the Mexican-American War erupted, however, he enlisted and quickly rose to the post of brigadier general.

As the 1852 Democratic convention approached, four candidates seemed serious contenders. After none had won a two-thirds majority on the thirty-fourth ballot, Pierce's name was introduced. The "dark horse" won the nomination on the forty-ninth ballot. Jane fainted at the news.

The Pierces had already lost two sons:

Franklin at three days old, Frank to typhus at age four. Two months before his inauguration, the president-elect and his wife witnessed the death of their third son, Bennie, when their train car derailed. He was eleven years old. "It is a relief to feel that no heart but my own can know the personal regret and bitter sorrow with which I have been borne to a position so suitable for others rather than desirable for myself," Franklin said in his inaugural address. Jane spent two years holed up on the White House's second

floor, penning letters to her dead son and blaming her husband.

The home where the president spent far happier years was acquired by the state in 1925 from Pierce descendants, and tours are offered by the Hillsborough Historical Society daily in July and August and weekends in June, September, and October. Pierce once reflected, "I shall never cease to remember my birthplace with pride as well as affection," and Hillsborough reciprocates by ensuring his tattered legacy is viewed within the context of his personal life and times.

Aspet House/Augustus Saint-Gaudens National Historic Site

139 Saint-Gaudens Road • Cornish, NH 03745 • 603-675-2175

www.nps.gov/saga

This Federal-style brick tavern, built circa 1800 in the Vermont–New Hampshire border town of Cornish, would be of little consequence had it not been reluctantly rented in 1885 by Augustus Saint-Gaudens. The tavern, christened "Huggins' Folly" by locals, failed miserably when traffic along Route 12A never surged, as projected. The subsequent brothel suffered an identical fate, and for seventy years, the building sat vacant. New York City attorney Charles C. Beaman purchased the property for a song in 1884 and enticed Saint-Gaudens, his client and friend, to take up summer residence by proclaiming the upper Connecticut River Valley a "land of Lincoln-shaped men."

The heralded sculptor indeed found a Vermont farmer to model for his latest commission, the *Standing Lincoln* for Chicago's Lincoln Park. Although Saint-Gaudens initially loathed country living, that prolific summer convinced him to flee the city annually and to purchase the estate in 1892; he named it Aspet for his father's French Pyrenees birthplace. The lanky, bearded redhead, who shot to fame when his first major work, a statue of Admiral David Farragut, was unveiled in 1881 in New York's Madison Square, was a Gilded Age household name. Each summer, when his artistic enterprise and cadre of assistants relocated to New Hampshire, other creative New Yorkers

followed. At its height, the Cornish Art Colony counted ninety members within a four mile radius: Aspet was its nucleus.

Paintings by fellow colonists Thomas Dewing and George de Forest Brush are among the home's collection of original furnishings and possessions. While brief tours encompass only the first floor, they offer insight into Saint-Gaudens's life and relationships. Gus met his wife, Augusta Homer, while studying in Rome, and although Gussie was a self-taught painter of some merit, she completed only a handful of canvases after they wed, focusing instead on raising a son, Homer, and shrewdly managing household and business affairs. An accomplished haggler, Gussie exploited her chronic tinnitus to ensure she never heard a price she didn't like: Aspet's décor reflects her thriftiness. Still, Gus invested in improving his retreat, adding a

curving interior stairway, dormers, and a columned piazza.

Conspicuously missing from the home's interior are any works by the celebrated sculptor, who began his career as a cameo carver and became as renowned for low-relief portraits and coin designs for the U.S. mint as for larger-than-life monuments. With his studios on-site, Augustus likely desired respite from his labors. Perhaps, also, the dreamlike face of Davida Clark—the mistress who bore Saint-Gaudens's second son and often inspired his figures—was verboten. As visitors explore the lovely grounds, however, they can spy more than one hundred Saint-Gaudens creations. Recast large-scale works, such as Boston's intricate Shaw Memorial honoring the Massachusetts Fifty-Fourth Regiment of African American Volunteers and the hauntingly beautiful Adams Memorial in

Washington, DC, commissioned by historian Henry Adams following his wife's suicide, are installed in contemplative natural spaces. At times cocky, at others insecure, Saint-Gaudens was relentlessly devoted to detail, as evinced by smaller works displayed inside galleries and the Little Studio, a 1904 structure featuring an enchanting vine-draped Saint-Gaudens-designed pergola.

From 1900 until his death in 1907, Saint-Gaudens made Cornish his year-round home. A cancer diagnosis in 1900 and studio fire in 1904 that destroyed priceless records and four years' work were devastating to the artist. Here, however, he lived to the fullest, playing ice hockey, constructing a toboggan run, and deriving strength from his craft and his colleagues, whom he treated with unflagging generosity. Gussie was never as fond of the parade of characters, especially since one of her home's

attractions was the town's first telephone, for which she paid the bill. Nevertheless, her 1919 decision to create a non-profit to administer the 150-acre property as a memorial to her husband was a most magnanimous gift.

The National Park Service acquired the site, which is open for tours daily from Memorial Day weekend through October, in 1966, forever preserving a place of rare inspiration. From the formal gardens to the allée of birches, the artist's genius is evident in the beloved landscapes he fashioned. A walk across what was formerly an irrigated nine-hole golf course to the Temple—built in 1905 for a theatrical tribute by Cornish Colony members and the place of interment for the family's ashes—reveals the lonely silhouette of Mount Ascutney looming against a cobalt sky. It's a scene that must have humbled even the American Michelangelo.

The Fells/John Hay
National Wildlife Refuge

456 Route 103A • Newbury, NH 03255 • 603-763-4789
www.thefells.org

"Saint-Gaudens is going to bust my head," wrote John Hay to his wife, Clara, in 1903. Although he deemed the sculptor's ten-thousand-dollar fee "a ruinous expense and folly," the statesman rationalized, "I have been a long time in office and only just now recognize that perhaps I may be considered a bust-worthy name in our annals." Indeed, Hay witnessed, influenced, and chronicled pivotal events in American history. The Midwesterner, educated at Rhode Island's Brown University, went to Washington, DC, at age twenty-two to serve as Abraham Lincoln's personal secretary. He was the sequestered president's eyes and ears on the capital's social scene and kept vigil beside his deathbed. After turns as Lincoln biographer, *New York Tribune* editor, and ambassador to the United Kingdom, Hay was named secretary of state by William McKinley and retained that post under Theodore Roosevelt following McKinley's assassination.

Hay's public persona had an alter ego, and it is the quiet, introspective poet who began buying up abandoned New Hampshire farms in 1888. In 1891, a country home was built on the thousand-acre summer estate Hay named The Fells, a Scottish term for rocky upland pastures. Railroad and steamboat transportation had made the Granite State's mountain breezes and sparkling waters accessible to a new class of vacationers, and the Hays welcomed a who's who of luminaries to their Lake Sunapee–side retreat, most notably President Roosevelt, who planted the front lawn's majestic maple in 1902. Here, John and Clara also grieved the death of eldest son Adelbert, who fell from a third-story window during his triennial reunion at Yale—just days before he was to become McKinley's assistant personal secretary.

Younger son Clarence, an ancient Mexico scholar and archaeologist, inherited the property after his father succumbed to a stroke at The Fells in 1905. His wife, Alice, was reportedly reduced to tears by the prospect of summering in this rugged, isolated spot. Gradually, however, the couple transformed The Fells into a gracious Colonial Revival estate. Architect Prentice Sanger refashioned the twenty-two-room main house, and Clarence, an amateur botanist, installed extensive gardens designed to provide an aesthetic transition between the home and surrounding regrowth forest. The sloping rock garden, added in the 1930s, features granite stepping stones, gravity-fed reflecting pools, and a colorful assemblage of more than six hundred species of alpine and other hardy plants. Formal gardens, including the Rose Terrace and one-hundred-foot perennial border, supplied the home with fresh flowers, which Alice enjoyed arranging.

By the time of her death in 1987, Alice's attitude toward The Fells was entirely altered. The couple had already donated 675 acres to the Society for the Protection of New Hampshire Forests prior to Clarence's death in 1969. Alice deeded the family home and 164 additional acres to the U.S. Fish and Wildlife Service, which established the John Hay National Wildlife Refuge. Unaccustomed to overseeing cultivated environments, the agency turned to the Garden Conservancy for landscape preservation assistance and transitioned ownership of the home and eighty-four acres to a non-profit friends organization.

Grounds, gardens, and woodland walking paths are open daily year-round; tours of the house and its galleries are offered Memorial Day weekend through Columbus Day. Because the home's contents were auctioned following Alice's death, rooms are furnished to approximate their early twentieth-century appearance with a mix of family possessions and period pieces. A portion of John Hay's book collection lines library shelves. The portrait above the dining room fireplace is of Alice, who was known for being rather particular: she'd be dismayed to see the maid's china prominently displayed. Among the exhibits in the guestroom where Roosevelt slumbered is a plaster cast on loan from the Augustus Saint-Gaudens National Historic Site. While Hay's political career may be the dusty stuff of history texts, his and his heirs' stewardship of this vast natural tract on Sunapee's shore is eminently bust-worthy.

Lucknow/Castle in the Clouds

Route 171, 455 Old Mountain Road • Moultonborough, NH 03254 • 603-476-5900
www.castleintheclouds.org

The drive to Castle in the Clouds is an exhilarating two-mile skyward climb, interrupted only by an obligatory stop a quarter-mile up for a two-hundred-yard hike to the soaring, sparkling Falls of Song. It's an allegorical ascent, reminiscent of owner Thomas Plant's meteoric rise, which peaked after a dalliance with a statuesque beauty. Marvelous views await at the top, where the impressive stone home, which took one thousand craftsmen more than a year to build, overlooks island-strewn Lake Winnipesaukee and the ancient volcanic Belknap and Ossipee mountains.

Born in 1859 in Bath, Maine, to a working-class French-Canadian family, Plant left to seek fortune at age fourteen. After stints as a boilermaker and ice cutter, he apprenticed at a shoe mill in Lynn, Massachusetts—the world's shoemaking capital. Self-educated and industrious, Plant owned a shoe company by age twenty-seven, secured several patents, and when he retired at fifty-one, his Jamaica Plain factory—one of five he owned—was the largest manufacturer of women's shoes in the world, with fifty-two hundred employees producing three million pairs annually. With a fortune estimated at twenty-one million dollars—the equivalent of one billion dollars today—Plant, who fell for a woman twenty-four years his junior while gallivanting in France in 1912, could afford to slip a one-million-dollar check inside his wife Caroline's napkin ring one morning before breakfast and sashay out the door.

Lucknow, as they named their mountaintop hideaway on sixty-three hundred lush acres, was a wedding gift for Plant's young bride, Olive Cornelia Dewey. Designed by Boston architects J. Williams Beal & Sons, the Arts and Crafts–style castle and carriage house were constructed of granite quarried from the property and handcut by Italian masons—at a rate of about three stones each per day. Self-guided tours, offered early May through mid-October, allow visitors to wander

the mansion's grand yet inviting rooms, with their dramatic views and mostly original furnishings, including many pieces custom-made by Irving & Casson-A.H. Davenport, Boston's leading furniture makers.

Like any good castle, Lucknow has its share of gizmos and surprises. The brine refrigerator in the butler's pantry was chilled by an innovative saltwater system in the basement. The central vacuum was a rare luxury in 1914. Bathrooms are out-fitted with Needle surround showers—a complex plumbing apparatus for the day. The main hall's Aeolian pipe organ could be played manually or via player scrolls. Its booming chords were overheard by boaters on the lake below. A petite suit of armor in the office, reportedly worn by Plant to a masquerade, and the portrait of Napoleon in the library hint at Plant's diminutive stature. At five feet, Plant could easily duck through the short door to his secret room off the library, confident that six-foot-tall Olive could not intrude.

Less of a cad than he may seem, Plant had been a benevolent, progressive employer, who shortened factory workers' hours and provided amenities ranging from recreational facilities to noontime concerts. His first wife wanted for little after his departure. But Plant's luck changed shortly after his remarriage. He invested in Russian bonds … just before the 1917 Russian Revolution. He bought Cuban sugar futures … then a

hurricane wiped out the crop. He lost more in the 1929 stock market crash. All but one household employee was let go. When the master bedroom balcony was destroyed by a hurricane, the Plants could not afford repairs. By 1940, although Thomas and Olive were allowed to remain, the property was owned by creditors. The next summer, three days after receiving notice the estate would be auctioned, the heirless eighty-two-year-old Plant died. He was so broke, friends chipped in for his burial expenses.

Subsequent owners bestowed the Castle in the Clouds moniker and tapped the estate's lumber and spring water resources, as well as its tourist potential. In 2001, the Lakes Region Conservation Trust purchased this unique architectural landmark and fifty-four hundred exquisite acres crisscrossed by forty-five miles of carriage-road hiking trails from the Castle Springs bottling company. The non-profit trust's subsidiary, the Castle Preservation Society, is actively raising five million dollars to restore the structure ahead of its 2014 centenary.

From the castle lawn, the view is all downhill to the jagged shores of Winnipesaukee, and, like Thomas Plant, a dramatic descent is in store for those who visit this exalted spot. Yet, Lucknow's fortunes are looking up, and preservation efforts ensure the shoe tycoon's greatest legacy will have generations of appreciative heirs.

Moffatt-Ladd House & Garden

154 Market Street • Portsmouth, NH 03801 • 603-436-8221 • 603-430-7968
www.moffattladd.org

The Moffatt-Ladd House is a fine example of Georgian architecture, a testament to the skills of colonial craftsmen, a stop on Portsmouth's Black Heritage Trail, and the former home of one of America's Founding Fathers. Its terraced Colonial Revival garden provides blissful respite from urban frenzy. Its colossal horse chestnut—listed on the National Register of Historic Trees—has shaded the home's hilltop plot for centuries: It was planted by General William Whipple and his enslaved servant, Prince, with a chestnut that the Declaration of Independence signer tucked into a pocket before returning from Philadelphia in 1776. The still-active wharves on the Piscataqua River below and the widow's walk atop Portsmouth's first three-story home hint at the source of the Moffatt family fortune.

John Moffatt, a sea captain, merchant, and land speculator, was one of New Hampshire's wealthiest colonists by the time he decided to build a home overlooking his wharves. No expense was spared in constructing this gift for his son, Samuel, and his bride, Sarah Catherine Mason. Alas, within four years after occupying this elegant residence in 1763, Samuel's disastrous dealings and lavish spending had plunged them into debt so extreme that he was forced to flee to the West Indies. Sarah Catherine followed, leaving her home and youngest two children in the care of Samuel's sister, Katharine.

Within a year of inheriting her nephew and niece, Katharine also welcomed her widowed father and married Whipple, whose slave, Prince, likely shared the household servants' third-floor quarters. As Whipple became embroiled in the colonial cause, Prince was at his side, both in military service and at the Continental Congress, where impassioned debate resulted in the removal of language condemning slavery from Thomas Jefferson's initial draft. In 1779, Prince Whipple and nineteen fellow "natives of Africa, now forcibly detained" petitioned the

New Hampshire legislature for their freedom. Although their eloquent, well-articulated plea was not granted, the general freed his trusted companion in 1784.

Following the deaths of William Whipple in 1785 and the elderly John Moffatt in 1786, the home's ownership became the subject of complex and divisive legal wranglings between Samuel's heirs and Katharine Whipple. By the time the matter was settled, Portsmouth's status as a major tradeport had drastically diminished, as had the mansion's value. In 1819, John Moffatt's great-granddaughter, Maria Tufton Haven, whose mother, Polly, had been raised in the house by her Aunt Katharine, finally acquired the property with her husband, Alexander Ladd, for the sum of one dollar.

Their son, Alexander Hamilton Ladd, expanded the garden and made updates while preserving the structure's most distinctive features during his 1862–1900 tenure. Eleven years after his death, Ladd's children, keenly aware of their father's passion for his ancestral home, offered it to the state chapter of the National Society of the Colonial Dames of America. It opened as a museum in 1912.

Visitors who tour the Moffatt-Ladd House mid-June through mid-October see a blend of family possessions, reproductions, and furnishings collected by the Dames: Rooms represent various periods in the family's history. The vast entry hall, with its

curved banister, turned balusters, and wood-work elaborately carved by Ebenezer Dearing, is as striking as when colonial notables gathered here. The Yellow Chamber appears as it did in 1768, when Sarah Catherine gave birth to Polly. The dining room, with its Portsmouth-made inlaid furniture, reflects the Ladds' early nineteenth-century taste. An assortment of well-loved playthings is exhibited on the third floor.

Items in the collection range from the quirky to the sublime. A Moule Earth Commode, patented in 1869, was a luxury installed by Alexander Hamilton Ladd. It's easy to understand why this dirt-powered

sanitary device lost out to the rival water closet. A partial set of Chinese Chippendale mahogany furniture crafted in London circa 1760, acquired by the family at an estate sale in 1794, is believed to have belonged to royal governor John Wentworth. And outdoors in the captivating garden, with its winding paths and intimate compartments, an English damask rose planted in 1768 by Sarah Catherine Moffatt—who returned to Portsmouth following Samuel's death in 1780 to find she'd been excluded from her father-in-law's will—still thrives and blooms.

Wentworth-Coolidge
Mansion Historic Site

375 Little Harbor Road • Portsmouth, NH 03801 • 603-436-6607
www.nhstateparks.org; Search: Wentworth-Coolidge Mansion State Historic Site

He appointed his relatives and friends to influential positions, knowingly violated trade laws, schemed to sell property he didn't own, and kept a piece of the action whenever he made a grant. If that wasn't scandalous enough, the sixty-four-year-old married his twenty-three-year-old housemaid, raising eyebrows on two sides of the Atlantic. It reads like a tabloid tale of twenty-first-century political corruption and vice, but it's actually the story of Benning Wentworth, the first royal governor of New Hampshire.

The province was newly separated from Massachusetts when Wentworth took the reigns in 1741, and the crown's appointee profited immensely by deeding himself a five-hundred-acre plot within each of more than two hundred towns he doled out to supporters and developers. Wentworth even granted Vermont townships, including the self-named Bennington, in spite of New York's claim to the territory. The governor, who lost his first wife and three sons to diphtheria, further sullied his reputation by taking up with Martha Hilton, whose fairy-tale ascent to the status of richest woman in the province was immortalized in Henry Wadsworth Longfellow's poem "Lady Wentworth."

The forty-room mansion overlooking Portsmouth's Little Harbor, where the couple tied the knot in 1760, was part of the fortune Martha inherited when Wentworth died in 1770. Built by the governor circa 1755 on a spectacular hundred-acre gentleman's farm, the sprawling structure also housed the council chamber and government offices. An underground tunnel to the dock ensured the royal ruler could quickly flee to Fort William and Mary.

While the wood-frame house's mustard-painted, red-shingled exterior was repaired and refreshed in 2008, the interior leaves much to the imagination for visitors who tour

the state-owned historic site during the summer and fall. Furnishings are sparse, moisture damage is rampant, original eighteenth-century wallpapers are faded and frayed, and because Wentworth's papers were destroyed, much is left to conjecture. What lavish meals must have emerged from the French sauce kitchen, one of four food preparation rooms? What deals were struck across the billiard room's missing table? What tunes might Michael Wentworth—the governor's cousin and his young widow's second husband—have played on his harpsichord when he and Martha welcomed George Washington in 1789?

An upstairs passageway leads to the governor's secret sanctum, which is in the saddest shape of all. Despite its condition, the home—one of the most outstanding survivors from the period—conveys a sense of the grandeur that the colonial upper crust enjoyed. Within the echoing council chamber, with its elaborately carved, floor-to-ceiling mantel and reproduction of Joseph Blackburn's larger-than-life portrait of Benning Wentworth, one feels particularly ensconced in history. Although Longfellow's account was fictionalized, guests who'd gathered here for dinner probably *were* "greatly mystified" when Wentworth announced his intention to wed a servant girl.

Martha and Michael's daughter, Martha, was the last Wentworth to live in the home. Charles Cushing purchased the estate for

his family in 1816 and continued to operate the farm. His nephew, William Israel, who inherited the property in 1860, was the first to open its doors to curious tourists. In 1886, Israel sold the mansion and fifteen acres to John Templeman Coolidge, a Boston artist and antiquarian who was equally attuned to the building's significance. Coolidge consulted his friend Sumner Appleton, founder of the Society for the Preservation of New England Antiquities (now Historic New England), before restoring the home, which became the hub of a summer colony of writers and artists.

The estate's water views remain inspiring, and when lilac time arrives each May, the air is perfumed by flowering bushes descended from those Wentworth imported in the 1750s. A newspaper ad Israel ran is posted in the mansion's entryway: "A Most Interesting Old Mansion / Tourists, Attention! / Governor Wentworth's Homestead at Little Harbor."

Attention—and care—is what this interesting mansion most deserves.

Part VI
Maine

The Nott House

8 Maine Street • Kennebunkport, ME 04046 • 207-967-2751
www.kporthistory.org

Charles Edwin Perkins, whose grandfather founded a highly regarded Kennebunkport shipbuilding and trading company, was one of the wealthiest men in one of New England's most prosperous mid-nineteenth-century towns. That made him quite a catch for Celia Nott, the eldest of Reverend Handel Nott's sixteen children. The home Charles purchased from his father in 1853, newly enlarged and refashioned in Greek Revival style, was just steps from the Baptist church where Celia's father preached, but this grand edifice represented a quantum leap in lifestyle for his new bride.

Still, we know from Celia's daily jottings that her life was only semi-charmed. Standing in front of the Nott House, with its red-shingled roof, crisp black shutters, and powerfully plain Doric columns, it is easy to envision the mournful appearance the home took on twice in 1865. On April 19, five days after Abraham Lincoln's assassination, Celia wrote: "Our flag draped in black bunting hangs from the balcony." Later that year, she lamented: "The black bunting goes out again." Daughter Lela, a precocious child who'd learned to read English and French by age five, had contracted diphtheria at a neighbor's birthday party and perished at the age of ten. On August 14, 1877, nearly nine months after their second child, Charlie, was rescued from a frigid mill pond while ice skating, Celia's words portend the teen's tragic fate. "A bomb has burst in our midst," she inscribed, as Charlie succumbed to seizures and spells of delirium. He required constant care until his death at age twenty-nine.

The journals faithfully kept by Celia and two succeeding generations of Nott House women preserve the home's human story while also documenting everything from the purchase of specific furnishings to the more than one hundred plants that graced the Victorian-era garden, which was restored in 2003. In 1929, for example, third-generation owner Celia

Parker Nott, Charles and Celia's niece, wrote in her diary after acquiring a chandelier that hung in Handel Nott's church at an estate sale: "It's now in the dining room where it belongs."

The Kennebunkport Historical Society, which was deeded the mansion in 1982 by the last descendent to occupy the home, Elizabeth Nott, strives to maintain everything in its place. Elizabeth and her siblings, who had spent childhood summers visiting Kennebunkport, inherited the property when their aunt Celia died in 1955. After retiring to the seaport community, Elizabeth became an active member of the historical society. Fearing her ancestral home's location near Dock Square would destine it for commercial development, she donated the stately structure and its complete contents—including thirty-three artifact-filled trunks in the attic—to the non-profit for preservation.

Nott House tours, offered July through early October, allow visitors to see a remarkable collection of original furniture, rugs, wall coverings, clothing, and family heirlooms. While some rooms, such as the 1955 kitchen, reflect the fourth generation's occupancy, much remains from Celia and Charles's day, including their massive Michigan-made burled walnut bedroom set; the handprinted French wallpaper in the first-floor hall; their wedding china; and Lela and Charlie's playthings. Guests also glimpse a room that raised a few eyebrows when Charles installed it in 1886: Kennebunkporters weren't at all sure it was sanitary to bring the outhouse indoors.

Hamilton House

40 Vaughan's Lane • South Berwick, ME 03908 • 207-384-2454
www.historicnewengland.org; Search: Hamilton House

The Hamilton House described in the opening scenes of *The Tory Lover* only faintly resembles the South Berwick, Maine, mansion this 1901 historical romance's author, Sarah Orne Jewett, had cherished since her childhood. By the late nineteenth century, Colonel Jonathan Hamilton's "high house on the river bank" was badly deteriorated. Fortunately, Jewett was not alone in envisioning the bygone grandeur of this gracious Georgian overlooking the Salmon Falls River's tidal ripplings. When Bostonian Emily Tyson, widow of the president of the Baltimore and Ohio Railroad, and her stepdaughter visited the estate at the novelist's urging, they were similarly inspired. Although she first beheld the four-story house shrouded in snow on a bleak winter day, by March of 1898, Tyson wrote to her friend in South Berwick: "All our roads seem to lead us toward the Hamilton House."

At a time when rapid industrialization and urbanization were piquing nostalgia for simpler times, many Americans of means embraced the Colonial Revival movement, and the house built circa 1785 for Colonel Hamilton proved an ideal pet project for Emily and Elise Tyson. Until his death in 1802, Hamilton's shipping and shipbuilding enterprise had kept the waterfront below his home bustling with activity, but the Embargo Act of 1807, which shuttered America's ports to international trade, quieted traffic on New England's inland rivers. By 1839, the estate had its fifth owner. The fortunes of the Goodwins, who farmed the land for two generations, would also falter as rail transportation allowed agricultural products grown more cheaply in the Midwest to reach Northeastern markets.

The advent of railroads transformed southern Maine into a fashionable escape for wealthy summer vacationers like the Tysons, who set about refreshing Hamilton House to reflect their interpretation of Colonial charm and style. Visitors who step inside the front hall are immediately surrounded by one of the duo's most impressive undertakings: At the turn

of the twentieth century, it was not commonplace to reproduce antique wallcoverings, but the Tysons decked the hall with a faithful copy of the home's original 1780s wallpaper. Elise, a photography enthusiast who would later marry Henry Vaughan, documented the home's transformation, creating a valuable visual archive.

While many original features, including the brick hearth and impressive woodwork, were preserved, the Tysons did make changes. Two wings—one housing a modern kitchen—were added; plumbing was installed; and George Porter Fernald was hired in 1908 to paint fabulous murals, including a Mediterranean scene featuring a water line that appeared continuous with the river outside when seated guests gazed through dining room windows. Collections of ship models, maritime prints, colorful Sandwich glass, hand-hooked rugs, and Currier & Ives lithographs evoke the home's history. A bust of Benjamin Franklin and an engraving of a ship commanded by John Paul Jones—two of *The Tory Lover*'s prominent characters—reflect its literary legacy, although neither patriot ever set foot within its walls.

Vaughan, who continued to summer in South Berwick until her death in 1949, bequeathed the property to Historic New England, which offers tours of this Colonial Revival masterpiece, as well as the Sarah Orne Jewett House in downtown South Berwick, June through mid-October. While Hamilton House's wings were removed for the sake of architectural purity, another of the women's twentieth-century add-ons has been meticulously restored since 1997. The terraced, hedge- and rock wall–enclosed Colonial Revival garden blends colorful plantings and distinctive architectural features: weathered millstones, brick paths, a sundial, an arched pergola, and a garden cottage built in 1907 with reclaimed materials from an abandoned eighteenth-century New Hampshire home.

In 1929, a series of four *House Beautiful* stories touted the remarkable restoration of this riverside retreat. The magazine's vivid images and descriptions have helped Historic New England to recreate and interpret the house's 1920s heyday. While fashion and romanticism may have motivated Colonial Revival–era preservationists—more so than authenticity—for visitors who stroll this serene, off-the-beaten path haven, its benefactors' mission to conjure simpler times seems palpably complete.

The Wadsworth-Longfellow House

489 Congress Street • Portland, ME 04101 • 207-774-1822
www.mainehistory.org; Search: Wadsworth-Longfellow

A century before horror master Stephen King was born in Portland, Maine, the state's first bestselling writer, also a Portland son, published the piece that would catapult him to commercial success. By ten years after its release in 1847, the epic poem of lost love *Evangeline* had sold nearly thirty-six thousand copies—a far cry from the million copies of King's debut novel, *Carrie*, purchased the year the paperback was issued. Still, Henry Wadsworth Longfellow's literary success enabled him to retire from teaching at Harvard. Writing for a still wet-behind-the-ears nation, the beloved poet whose verse immortalized *The Courtship of Miles Standish* and *Paul Revere's Ride* was as adept at stirring patriotic sentiment and inventing legends as King has been at tingling spines.

The bright cheery home where Longfellow spent his formative years is a window into his earliest influences. A destination for Longfellow fans since it opened to the public as Maine's first historic house museum in 1901, the oldest extant structure on the Portland peninsula would be of architectural and historic importance even had it not been the prolific poet's boyhood residence. Built by Henry's maternal grandfather from 1785 to 1786 and expanded to three stories by his parents, Stephen and Zilpah Longfellow, after an 1814 chimney fire destroyed the roof, the Neoclassical-style house was the first entirely brick edifice in this coastal city.

From his bedroom window, Henry could observe ships sailing into Portland Harbor. Vivacious like his mother, whose own penchant for verse influenced her selection of names for her brood—Stephen and Henry, Eliz'beth and Anne, Alex and Mary, Ellen and Sam—the second eldest was "the sunlight of the house," according to his brother Samuel. Descended from nine *Mayflower* Pilgrims, the grandson of a comrade-in-arms of George Washington,

and the son of a prosperous lawyer and one-term congressman, Henry absorbed history simply by listening to family stories and observing his surroundings. He published his first poem in the *Portland Gazette* at age thirteen, graduated from Bowdoin College at eighteen, learned six languages during a three-year European tour, and became an esteemed professor of European languages, first at his alma mater, then at Harvard in 1834. Cambridge was Henry's home as his literary career flourished, the world showered him with honors, and his list of friends grew to resemble a nineteenth-century who's who, but he returned to his family homestead in Maine each summer.

Twice, the poet's sunlight was extinguished by tragic loss. His first wife, Mary Potter, died following a miscarriage when Henry was only twenty-eight. In 1861, his second wife and

mother of six, Fanny Appleton, caught fire while melting sealing wax and could not be saved, despite Henry's efforts to extinguish the flames. The Santa Claus–like beard the poet wore thenceforth gave him a sage's appearance, but it was primarily camouflage for the burns he sustained.

Although grief impacted the poet's work, it did not diminish his popularity, his social circle, or his eagerness to travel. His younger sister Anne's experience of tragedy was remarkably dissimilar, however. Anne lived all but three of her ninety years in the family's Portland home, which she inherited following the deaths of her mother and a maiden aunt. Married in 1832 to George Washington Pierce, a Bowdoin classmate of Henry's and law student of her father's, Anne was devastated when the husband she adored contracted typhus and left her widowed at

twenty-five. She never remarried, devoting her life to cultivating the garden, entertaining family, and eventually, to ensuring the legacy of her home.

Although she updated the house's décor in the 1850s, Anne did little to alter the structure or its fixtures. The kitchen's open hearth and brick bread oven survive. The outhouse is gone, although it had the dubious distinction of being the last one in use in Portland. "I do hate to change anything so much," Anne once wrote. Upon her death in 1901, she bequeathed the home to the Maine Historical Society. In 2002, a century after the Wadsworth-Longfellow House opened as one of America's earliest house museums, the society completed an extensive, well-researched restoration of the property to its 1850s appearance. Although ninety percent of the home's furnishings and artifacts

are original, many wall and floor coverings and textiles are reproductions. The Colonial Revival garden tucked behind the house was restored in 2009.

On tours, offered May through October, visitors see an array of intriguing artifacts, from the Washington jug the family filled with lemonade each Fourth of July to Henry's portable felt-top writing desk: the precursor to modern laptops. Henry postulated in "An Old Time Pottery": "All things must change / To something new, to something strange; / Nothing that is can pause or stay."

Dwarfed now by commercial development on Congress Street, the Wadsworth-Longfellow House challenges this assertion, and as the Declaration of Independence is read on the lawn each July 4, listeners sense that the American mythology the poet helped to originate will likewise surely endure.

Victoria Mansion

109 Danforth Street • Portland, ME 04101 • 207-772-4841
www.victoriamansion.org

The 1850s ushered in a new architectural era in America. As the classical lines and stark symmetry of the Greek Revival period became passé, Connecticut architect Henry Austin found his mastery of Italianate style in high demand. Situated on a peaceful residential street just blocks from the bustling commercial wharves in Maine's largest city, the brownstone-faced villa Austin designed for Ruggles Morse and his wife, Olive, remains one of the finest surviving examples of mid-nineteenth-century American architecture. Victoria Mansion's tall, slender windows; varied rooflines; decorative cornices; exaggerated eaves; boxy four-story tower; double columns; and gracious yet restrained entry porch make it a textbook example of Italianate form. Although the rosy brownstone, quarried in Portland, Connecticut, has required restorative measures, the home remains wondrously intact considering coastal Maine's harsh climate.

As the mansion's front doors shut with a resounding thud, visitors' first glimpses of the main hall's frescoed ceilings and walls, faux three-dimensional trompe l'oeil effects, vivid stained glass, and three-story walnut flying staircase elicits spontaneous "wows!" The ambiance is imposing, not comforting. The impressive gasolier—a gas-lit chandelier—seems out of place in a private home. Clues as to how Ruggles Morse amassed the money to erect the most costly residence built in Maine as of 1860 are immediately evident. The staircase landing's stained glass window depicts two state seals: Maine and Louisiana. Although he and his wife were native Mainers, Morse was a successful hotelier in the South's largest city: New Orleans. The couple visited their newly completed abode in 1860, but they could not resume summering in Portland until 1866, after the Civil War.

Victoria Mansion's interior spaces are not only reminiscent of a grand hotel; they display the energetic carnival of colors, textures, and patterns that characterized the Victorian period. The meticulously integrated floor-to-ceiling design of each of the themed rooms was the work of German immigrant Gustave Herter, who would build on the reputation earned from this first major commission. He went on to establish the prominent New York City interior design and furnishings firm Herter Brothers with his half brother, Christian. Herter's plan incorporated works of art collected by the Morses, fresco secco wall scenes painted by Giuseppe Guidicini, and more than one hundred furnishings and fixtures crafted at his own workshop. The most extraordinary Herter piece, a carved and inlaid rosewood and birdseye maple cabinet and desk, occupies a mysterious little chamber off the home's reception room.

Accustomed to providing the latest luxuries to hotel guests, Morse equipped his home with water closets, hot and cold running water, and a coal furnace. Upstairs, the dazzling Turkish Smoking Room, tucked behind jewel-toned, glass-adorned pocket doors, is America's oldest extant Islamic-influenced room and one of the earliest smoking parlors on record. Its ornate gasolier could be lowered to shed light on the gaming table.

In the main hall, guides point out that only three of the four virtues are depicted on the plastered ceiling. Missing is Temperance: Morse, of course, secured his fortune through wining and dining. Also conspicuously absent from the home are signs of children: The Morses had none of their own, and the young niece whose portrait hangs in the second-floor Red Bedroom died before the painting was completed. Shortly after her husband's death in 1893, Olive sold the mansion and the majority of its contents to Portland businessman Joseph Ralph Libby. He, his wife, and their five children were gentle with the treasure they'd acquired during their thirty-five-year occupancy. Although the Libby children removed some pieces in 1928, they and their descendants have returned many to the home.

The result is that Victoria Mansion's original décor is ninety percent complete. The preservation of the home, a National Historic Landmark since 1971, is also owed to William H. Holmes, who purchased it in 1940 and, with his sister Clara's assistance, opened it as a museum. In 1943, the Victoria Society of Maine Women assumed ownership, and its successor non-profit sustains this Victorian gem, where tours are offered May through October and late November through early January.

The Morses' palatial, if impersonal, Portland house was contrived to flaunt one Mainer's wealth. A century and a half later, it is a richly cherished city landmark—especially during the holiday season, when its lavish interiors are graced with flowers, baubles, and Maine evergreen.

Skolfield-Whittier House

161 Park Row • Brunswick, ME 04011 • 207-729-6606
www.community.curtislibrary.com/pejepscot.htm

Along Park Row, which flanks the green expanse of Brunswick's town mall, the Skolfield-Whittier House is one of several gracious dwellings built in the mid-nineteenth century by elite residents of this shipbuilding center and college town. Unlike Bowdoin graduates Henry Wadsworth Longfellow, Nathaniel Hawthorne, and Franklin Pierce, and professor's wife Harriet Beecher Stowe, who penned *Uncle Tom's Cabin* during her time in Brunswick, the Skolfields only achieved local prominence. Yet their home is an uncommon curiosity.

Although it appears to be one edifice, a walk around back reveals that two distinct houses share a streetside brick façade. Wealthy shipbuilder George Skolfield built the duplex for his sons, Alfred and Samuel, between 1858 and 1862. It is the home's southern side—occupied by sea captain Alfred and his descendants—that fascinates visitors. Inside, teapots in the china pantry sink appear as though they're being readied for afternoon company. The kitchen's coal-fired 1907 Magee Grand cast-iron stove looks surprisingly new. Frank Whittier's calling card is tucked inside a hall stand drawer, even though it's been more than a century since he courted the captain's eldest daughter, Eugenie. Threads and scraps from projects in process spill from a bedroom cabinet, and antique toiletries are haphazardly scattered on bathroom surfaces. In the dark, masculine, mid-Victorian-period sitting room, a mounted deer head surveys a scene that is unaltered—save for one missing painting—since 1888, when the captain and his family were photographed here.

One would require Goldilocks's bravado to lounge on the wicker fainting couch in the green room, to open the tin can of Pacific peanut butter, or indeed to disturb a thing among the eclectic collections and souvenirs proudly displayed. Not only does it appear as though

the inhabitants, who largely abandoned the home in 1925, might at any moment return, their possessions, although barely used, have been rendered fragile through decades of subtle deterioration. Only the drawing room, which even the family reserved for special occasions such as Alfred's wake and Eugenie and Frank's wedding just weeks later, seems to have dodged time's ravages.

A closer examination of the second-generation owners' story sheds light on the home's state of suspended animation. Eugenie, who studied in England during her family's two decades abroad and made more than twenty Atlantic crossings as a young woman, was exceedingly well-traveled and educated for a woman of her era. Frank, a hard-working physician and professor at his alma mater Bowdoin's medical school, was a pioneer in the study of forensics, who testified at murder trials using innovative techniques for examining blood and ballistic evidence. After Frank's death in 1924, Eugenie, who outlived him by twenty-seven years, shuttered the Park Row home and resumed her travels, perhaps to also escape reminders of their youngest daughter, Charlotte, who'd perished in 1912 at the age of nine when her frock caught fire on the kitchen stove.

Although Eugenie and her two eldest daughters returned to Brunswick for summer vacations, the home was never again occupied year-round. Educated and independent like their mother, the Whittier girls pursued careers: Isabel as a professor of history at Hunter College and Brooklyn College, Alice as Maine's first female pediatrician. Neither married. Although their Brunswick summer visits continued, and some modern items were purchased, almost nothing was removed or replaced.

In 1982, a dozen years before her death at the age of ninety-six, Alice donated her family's home to the Pejepscot Historical Society with instructions for the preservation of its contents. The society's offices occupy Samuel's side, and public tours of the attached treasure trove are offered during the summer and early fall. The final stop—the drawing room—provides an immersive glimpse of Victorian life, yet there is something bittersweet about this life-sized time capsule. Unfinished books stacked on chairs await their readers' return. And the candles in the chandelier—which Frank insisted remain dark at his 1895 wedding, and saved, in case his children would one day marry beneath their glow—have never been lit.

Suggested Readings

Batinski, Michael C. *Pastkeepers in a Small Place: Five Centuries in Deerfield, Massachusetts.* Amherst, MA: University of Massachusetts Press, 2004.

Beckius, Kim Knox, and William H. Johnson (photographer). *Backroads of New England: Your Guide to New England's Most Scenic Backroad Adventures.* Stillwater, MN: Voyageur Press, 2004.

Blackburn, Roderic H., and Geoffrey Gross (photographer). *Great Houses of New England.* New York, NY: Rizzoli, 2008.

Butler, Joyce, et. al. *Henry Wadsworth Longfellow and His Portland Home.* Portland, ME: Maine Historical Society, 2004.

Craven, Wayne. *Gilded Mansions: Grand Architecture and High Society.* New York, NY: W.W. Norton & Company, Inc., 2008.

Downing, A.J. *The Architecture of Country Houses.* New York, NY: Dover Publications, 1969.

Dryfhout, John H. *The Work of Augustus Saint-Gaudens.* Hanover, NH: University Press of New England, 2008.

Emmet, Alan. *So Fine a Prospect: Historic New England Gardens.* Hanover, NH: University Press of New England, 1996.

Epstein, David, and Michael Hubley (photographer). *Gardens of New England.* Rockport, MA: Twin Lights Publishers, 2008.

Foster, Gerald. *American Houses: A Field Guide to the Architecture of the Home.* New York, NY: Houghton Mifflin Company, 2004.

Garvin, James L. *A Building History of Northern New England.* Hanover, NH: University Press of New England, 2002.

Howard, Hugh, and Roger Straus III (photographer). *Houses of the Founding Fathers.* New York, NY: Artisan, 2007.

MacLeish, A. Bruce. *Rough Point: The Newport Home of Doris Duke.* Newport, RI: Newport Restoration Foundation, 2003.

McCullough, David. *John Adams.* New York, NY: Simon & Schuster, 2001.

Nylander, Jane C. *Our Own Snug Fireside: Images of the New England Home, 1760–1860.* New Haven, CT: Yale University Press, 1994.

Nylander, Jane C., and Diane L. Viera. *Windows on the Past: Four Centuries of New England Homes.* New York, NY: Bulfinch Press, 2000.

Pearson, Carmen. *The Collected Writings of Beatrix Farrand: American Landscape Gardener, 1872–1959.* Hanover, NH: University Press of New England, 2009.

Smith, A.G. *Historic Houses of New England Coloring Book.* New York, NY: Dover Publications, 1993.

Ward, Barbara McLean. *The Moffatt-Ladd House: From Mansion to Museum.* Portsmouth, NH: Moffatt-Ladd House & Garden, 2007.

Wharton, Edith, and Ogden Codman Jr. *The Decoration of Houses.* New York, NY: Cosimo Classics, 2008.

Yarnall, James. *Newport Through Its Architecture: A History of Styles from Postmedieval to Postmodern.* Newport, RI: Salve Regina University/University Press of New England, 2005.

Index

About the
Author & Photographer

Kim Knox Beckius

Kim Knox Beckius grew up in Hyde Park, New York, where playing on the lawns of spectacular historic mansions is something kids take for granted. She became particularly enchanted with the stories these homes have to tell while working as a tour guide at the Staatsburgh State Historic Site during her junior year in high school. After graduating from Marist College with a degree in history and communications, she served for a time as Education/Program Coordinator for Historic Hudson Valley at Montgomery Place in Annandale-on-Hudson, New York.

She relocated to Connecticut in 1996 and soon began sharing the wonders of her new home with a global audience via the New England Travel website she produces for About.com, a New York Times Company. At http://gonewengland.about.com, she takes Internet users on virtual tours, offers candid reviews, and provides lively weekly commentary on travel and events in the region.

Beckius's previous books include *The New England Coast: The Most Spectacular Sights & Destinations*, *The Everything Family Guide to New England*, *Backroads of New England*, and *Backroads of New York*. Her writing and photography have also been featured on several other websites and blogs, as well as in magazines. She is frequently called on by television, radio, and print media outlets to discuss travel and events in New England.

Although they have their most memorable family moments when they're on the road, Beckius, her husband Bruce, and their eight-year-old daughter are happy to call a remodeled and expanded 1880 farmhouse in Avon, Connecticut, home.

William H. Johnson

William H. Johnson is a native New Englander who lives in the Lakes Region of New Hampshire in an old restored farmhouse with his cat, Mittens. For over thirty years, his artistic landscapes have captured the spectacular New England countryside in all seasons. His work has been published in magazines, books, calendars, cards, puzzles, and advertising.

He studied photography at the Layton School of Art and Design in Milwaukee, Wisconsin, and the Doscher Country School of Photography in South Woodstock, Vermont. He was named Photographer of the Year by the New Hampshire Professional Photographers Association and has earned several Court of Honor awards.

Johnson has finally given in to the digital age and is no longer shooting film. All images were shot with a Nikon D300, as fourteen-bit raw files on a tripod using mirror lock-up method. He is still striving for quality images after all these years.

Photograph Permissions

Union Park Press wishes to thank all the historic homes featured in this book for their cooperation.

All images copyright William H. Johnson.

Images on pages 12-17; Henry Whitfield House, courtesy of the Connecticut Commission on Culture & Tourism.

Images on pages 18-23, Eolia Mansion at Harkness Memorial State Park; courtesy of Connecticut Department of Environmental Protection State Parks Division.

Images on pages 30-35; courtesy of The Mark Twain House & Museum, Hartford, CT.

Images on pages 36-41; courtesy of Historic New England and
Roseland Cottage, Woodstock, CT.

Images on pages 56-63; photographs by William H. Johnson of exteriors & interiors of The Breakers decorated for Christmas courtesy The Preservation Society of Newport County.

Images on pages 64-69; Rough Point, A Newport Restoration Foundation Property.

Images on pages 90-95; courtesy of the Bryant Homestead, The Trustees of Reservations.

Images on pages 118-125; courtesy of Naumkeag, The Trustees of Reservations.

Images on pages 188-193; courtesy of The Moffatt-Ladd House and Garden, Portsmouth, NH.

Images on pages 195-199; Wentworth-Coolidge Mansion Historical Site, courtesy State of New Hampshire.

Images on pages 206-211; courtesy of Historic New England and Hamilton House.

Images on pages 218-221; courtesy of Victoria Mansion
(The Morse-Libby House), Portland, ME.